THE W[ ]
OF GLORY

91ST

INFANTRY DIVISION

363RD

INFANTRY REGIMENT

BONNIE L. CARROLL

TURNER PUBLISHING COMPANY

DEDICATION

To my wife Delorah, who sent those sweet letters of love and affection through the mail service. She was a true lifeline of love, a source of inspiration and strength that kept this Infantry combat soldier living another day.

To Delorah's cousin, Flodell Tarr, who wrote often and told me about the whole world in just a few words. She wrote great letters. Thanks, Flodell, for the memories.

There is nothing more refreshing and rejoicing to the human soul than receiving a sweet loving letter from home.

There is nothing more disturbing to a person than when he doesn't get that letter from home that he was so eagerly expecting. He knew that he might not live to read tomorrow's mail.

Turner Publishing Company

Turner Publishing Company
Editor: Randy W. Baumgardner

Copyright © 1997, Bonnie L. Carroll
Publishing rights: 1999, Turner Publishing Company.
All rights reserved. Additional copies may be
purchased directly from Turner Publishing Company.

Library of Congress Catalog
Card Number: TXU 824-949
ISBN: 978-1-68162-407-5
Limited Edition.

ACKNOWLEDGMENTS

My heart is sad, and I send condolences to all of the families of the Infantry combat soldiers that made the great sacrifice. Also, I honor those who were seriously wounded and made it home safely, but have had to suffer through life.

This book is written to tell the real story of Company G, and to record some of the history and sacrifices that our men made during this great Italian campaign. This story has gone untold all of these years until now.

Special acknowledgment goes to Sergeant McDermott for his patience with me. For his true blue Infantry skills. He was a man with special vision, capable of sensing out danger when other GI's walked right out into the field of machine gun fire and were cut to pieces.

But for him it was "No sweat". He made the charge on the enemy when the time was always just right. With his sense of timing and outstanding shooting ability, he was awesome.

Special acknowledgement and many thanks to:

The Infantry Journal Press, for use of the War Department battlefield legends, and battlefield causality list being depicted in the book by Captain Strootman, *History Of The 363rd Regiment,* 1947. This information has been most helpful, enabling me to trace my footsteps through the rough and rugged terrain of the Apennine mountains as an infantry combat soldier.

Sincerely,

Bonnie L. Carroll

TABLE OF CONTENTS

TABLE OF CONTENTS

PREFACE

Private Bonnie Carroll, 1944

How does any person in his right mind wind up in the Infantry? Nobody will ever know if I don't tell you how I managed to fall into this death trap like millions of others. I was just barely 19 years old, married to a country farm girl, but couldn't get a farm deferment. I kept putting it off, and every time I was ready to volunteer into the Air Force, something always went wrong and I would change my mind.

The first time I decided to volunteer, I had gotten as far as Marietta, Oklahoma, when word was received that an acquaintance of mine, David Roberson, was killed in an aircraft training accident. He landed short of the runway and fell into the Puget Sound Bay in the State of Washington and killed instantly. The shock from that accident turned me off. About 30 days later, I was ready to volunteer once again, and guess what. Another acquaintance, Navy Aircraft Pilot Charles W. Reed, was killed while fighting Japanese Zero's in the battle of the Coral Sea. Again, that really turned me off. So I kept putting it off to the last minute and got caught in the draft like millions of others just like me.

At the time, I knew I had a hearing impairment but I was living in the country where no ear, eye, and nose specialist existed. I didn't have a chance to really identify my problem. However, after 40 years I finally found out that my real problem was a severe high frequency hearing loss. When drafted I went for my final physical at Fort Sill, Oklahoma, and I told the doctor that I had a hearing loss, but nobody listened. The doctor said, "Move on to the next position, soldier."

The next day we loaded onto Greyhound buses and given box lunches. We headed south to Wichita Falls, Texas, then down to Jacksboro, Texas. Then the bus turned back north, to just south of Dallas, and headed east to Tyler, Texas, the home of Camp Fanning (IRTC) Infantry Replacement Training Center. The camp was located about 20 miles outside of Tyler city limits, deep in the boondocks.

After 17 weeks of hard infantry training, I became a full fledged infantry rifleman. However, after all that training, I never did consent to being a rifleman. I hated it from the very beginning; but, what can you do about it? God only knows who will make a good rifleman and who won't. You will have to read the Biblical story of Gideon, to find out how God picked his army to really understand how Uncle Sam can get full utilization out of military men. I will attempt to summarize the Biblical story later in this book.

Camp Fanning was where I had the opportunity to meet my real combat buddies, Henry Ford Bowen and John R. Burklow. We left Camp Fanning by bus and hauled into Tyler, where we unloaded and later loaded onto a military passenger train. Destination, New Port News, where we waited for shipment overseas. The ship was a few days late, so we had some extra time to kill. We went on leave for a day and we had a choice of going to Washington D.C. or Boston. We three chose Boston. We got to see Boston Harbor and other historical sites around the city.

FOREWORD

The Soldier That Didn't Blink

Sgt. James L. McDermott attacked German pillboxes and machine gun nests like a tom cat on a June bug. When a German machine gunner opened up, we hit the dirt and waited for Sgt. McDermott to make the judgment call. We never questioned his ability. Obviously he knew exactly what to do. Of course, we knew what was coming next. Seven rounds of mortar fire came right in on top of us. The machine gunfire alerted the German mortar crew to commence firing at once because we were in the middle of the mortar's impact zone.

Sgt. McDermott would determine right off the bat just what type of enemy we were up against. For instance, if the machine gunner's fire went over our heads and was sporadic then Sgt. McDermott would call out, "He's a Pollock! Let's move on up cautiously and he will come out with his hands up over his head just as soon as he realizes that we got his message." If the machine gunner's fire directed right at us and at a very high rate of continuous firing, the soldier was a young German that was out to kill us at all cost.

Sgt. McDermott would call out, "Hold your fire, spread out and start firing into his position to draw attention away from me." Meanwhile, he was getting in a better position where he could nail him the next time he rose up to fire. "Bang." That was the end of that enemy machine gunner. One shot always did the trick. In other situations, the young German machine gunner would use up all of his ammo trying to kill us. Then the gunner would go out of his foxhole the back way trying to escape. That was the wrong thing for him to do because Sgt. McDermott had already set his sights on his escape route. "Bang." His helmet would roll.

The old Nazi-type German machine gunner was more clever with his firing. He would fire into our squad and keep us pinned down for the long haul, firing only when he saw a target to fire on. He was very conservative with his ammo, using the single shot method, squeezing off the trigger, and in some instances trying to pull out after he had done his damage. However, Sgt. McDermott was smart and knew what to do if he tried to pull out while we were attacking his position. Sgt. McDermott would look for a small flash of movement and that's all he needed to make the kill. One shot and the German's helmet would roll.

After the skirmish had finished Sgt. McDermott would call out, "Let's move out, men." HO-HUM. That sounds like a very simple matter, doesn't it? It only happens that way because Sgt. McDermott's marksmanship made it happen that way. At 100 yards, it was dead eye for him. He didn't have

Company G 363rd Infantry
Honor Goes Out To Our Platoon Leader
Sgt. James L. McDermott

to aim. He fired by open sight method. Our squad would attack pillboxes and bunkers the same way, but more dramatically. Sergeant would call in for close artillery support, and while the shells were still bursting on the enemy bunker-keeping them pinned down, Sergeant would start the attack.

He would have us get in as close to the enemy as possible before our artillery lifted, and then he would move in, quickly, with his rifle-blazing fire. He would then toss a live hand grenade inside the bunker to make the kill. Very seldom did we take prisoners during this critical moment. He was very careful about making every shot count. Not only was he careful, but extremely accurate with his shooting. I must say, these two important factors alone won our company many battles and saved many lives. Our most honorable mention goes to Sgt. McDermott. Thanks, sergeant, you did a great job.

Chapter 1
OCEAN VOYAGE

About the third day out, some of us were lying up in our bunks and others were playing poker when this old colonel came through our compartment. Nobody jumped up and brought us to attention, and that's when the old colonel had his aid write us up for Kitchen Police (K.P.) duty for the next 14 days aboard ship. Whoa, what a sweaty, messy job that was, washing pots and pans in the bottom of the ship. This was truly slave labor-type work, but top brass says this type of work makes men out of boys. You can believe that statement if you like; but for me, I thought five days in that hot kitchen below deck was enough punishment for the crime. However, what I thought didn't matter, so we went right on washing pots and pans for the rest of the trip.

After 15 days on the high seas, we turned into the Mediterranean Sea and knew at that moment our destination was the Italian Campaign. After a couple more days aboard ship, we finally reached our destination, Naples, Italy. We remained on ship until the next morning and orders came down to be ready to move off the ship within the next four hours. I walked out on deck and noticed a large crowd of people gathering along the dock area. They were ready to greet us as we departed the ship and to welcome us to their devastated city.

I noticed the children running alongside the GIs, jumping up on them as they entered the street below. As I entered the street, a youngster jumped upon me, locked his legs around me, and began to remove my cigarette packs from my ammo belt. He had about half of my cigarettes stolen before I realized what he was doing. He jumped off of my side and targeted another GI with an ammo belt full of cigarettes and jumped upon him and began to strip his cigarettes as well. This continued until all the GIs were off of the ship.

They herded us into a large assembly area to wait for the big truck convoy to come in and transport us up the highway to our first big stop, the famous Mussolini Dairy Farm. We spent two days there at the farm before we started our trek up the boot of Italy, in the back of a big, hot, dusty, GI truck. We were Infantry replacement soldiers looking for a home. We were willing to take a job from anybody who had an opening. A few days later, after the battle for Pisa and the Leaning Tower was over, we found our home. We were all three placed. I went to Co. G, Henry Bowen and John Burklow went to Co. E, 2nd Bn. 363rd Inf. We stayed in touch with each other until the Battle of Monticelli Ridge. That's where my friend John R. Burklow met his death and Henry F. Bowen got wounded. I survived this onlslaught and toughed it out until the end of the war.

Chapter 2
BATTLE FOR PISA AND LEANING TOWER

The 363rd Inf. Reg. came on line below Livorno (Leghorn) and entered Pisa where Co. G began to engage in heavy combat. This was where Co. G received their first heavy casualties. Sgt. McDermott[1]* and other men in the company told me about the battle for Pisa, just after being assigned to their unit.

Co. G was pinned down on the outskirts of Pisa. The second squad was inside the soccer stadium when they realized that the Germans were using the Leaning Tower as an Observation Post and were directing mortar fire right down the back of their necks. Co. G men all up and down the line began to call out for artillery fire be directed on the Tower. The GIs could see the Germans running around on the top deck of the Tower. They wanted to put a stop to that looking down their throats. Word came back that the Tower was

Leaning Tower of Pisa – taken in 1958, this was a favorite German observation post.

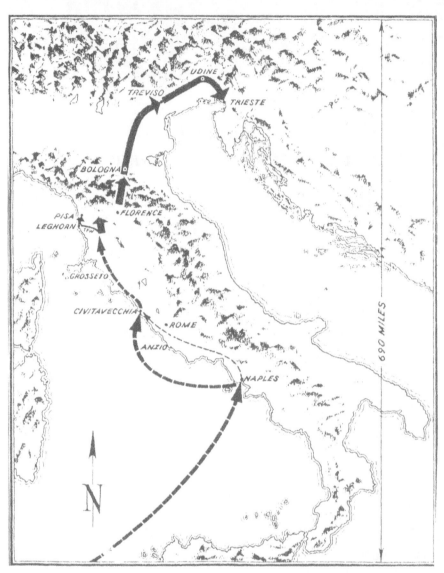

Route of the 363d Infantry

considered a historical site and was off limits to bombing and shelling. WOW! What a bunch of mad guys! They become fit to be tied over that decision. You know how it is. You put your life on the line every day in combat and then you come up against an object or a damn thing like this. Guess what! Top brass put historical value over human life. You could not believe it; but it was true.

Anyway, Co. G finally worked around this obstacle with the sacrifice of only a couple of GIs dead. What the heck, two GIs dead for something like this! The tower will probably stand for 200 years or more before it tumbles over, but the human soul will live for ever. I think this is a good scenario for this episode, don't you?

Co. G crawled out of this big mess and moved on into the main street of Pisa, where the firefights got hot and heavy. The first casualties received by the second squad were right here on the main street of Pisa, fighting house to house and door to door. The second squad was receiving heavy sniper and machine gunfire from the second floor of a building just a couple of blocks down the street.

Sgt. McDermott's men were taking cover in the doorway of houses as they advanced down the street. Pvt. Stern, the GI I later replaced, was advancing along a wall and decided to step inside the doorway leading into a house to avoid the heavy sniper fire that was coming his way. When he turned the doorknob, the building blew up in his face, killing him instantly. This was the first casualty our squad had suffered from what Uncle Sam identifies as a booby trap.[2]

The second squad knocked off the sniper and moved on down the street to the railroad tracks that went across the Arno River and led into the main German defense lines. It was dark by the time the squad got to the river and the Germans had the "choo-choo" rail lines zeroed in with heavy machine gunfire. Every time a GI got out of the bar ditch and started crawling across the rail lines, the Germans would open up with machine gunfire, playing havoc with the second squad.

However, after a long struggle trying to out-smart the machine gunner, they did make it over the tracks later on that night with two GIs casualties, both receiving flesh wounds in the butt. The battle of Pisa was over with. The 363rd Inf. Reg. moved over to the East, facing the city of Florence. During this time the whole 5th Army was holding along the Arno River. Meanwhile, we were moving up the boot of Italy in the back of a big, dusty, GI truck.

We were sweating it out, which includes Hank Bowen, John Burklow[3] and myself. We left Naples and went north to the famous Benito Mussolini Dairy Farm, waiting for our assignment to our regular unit.

Endnotes numbered 1 - 23 are placed in back of the book for your convenience.

Chapter 3
FIRST DAYS OF COMBAT

Later in the week we moved north once again and caught up with the 91st Inf. Div. 363rd Reg. 2nd Bn., Co. G where I was assigned. Co. G was in a holding position when I reported in for combat duty on a Saturday morning. The company was dug in along a ridge line above a small village right behind a Catholic Church that sat atop a small hill.

I reported in to the command post and Sgt. McDermott came down and picked me up. He took me back to the outpost, showed me around the area and got me acquainted with all my new combat buddies. Sgt. McDermott told me that this was my new home, and I was to dig in and make myself comfortable. The next morning, Sunday, everything was quiet on the front lines.

Sgt. McDermott came by and wanted to show me the exact spot where the company medic was killed the day before during a German Mortar attack. This one mortar round came in and hit the medic right in the middle of his back, blowing him into a million pieces. The only thing left of him to be found anywhere, was a little thread of cloth hanging in the very top of an old olive tree that stood nearby.

Sgt. McDermott went on to tell me what a brave soldier the medic was. He said on several occasions he was cited for bravery. For instance, he went out under heavy small arms and mortar fire and administered first aid to dying GIs without any fear whatsoever of being hit himself. One time he pulled his own medic's helmet off under heavy enemy fire. He then picked up a wounded GIs helmet and flopped it on his head and then grabbed the wounded GIs rifle and began to fire right into the German position.

This heroic action helped the remaining few GIs stave off a fierce German counterattack. Dead hero though he was, the action of this great soldier earned him the bronze star.

Later on that evening my new combat buddy, Irwin Motner, was heavily engaged in a big poker game when our artillery (105mm) opened up and fired two rounds of propaganda shells over into enemy territory. The shells went plop-plop and out came hundreds of propaganda leaflets that began to drift to the ground.

The wind just happened to pick up a little bit and some of them were floating over into our lines. Since Motner was too busy (tied up in a big poker game) he asked me to run out and pick up a few leaflets for him. When I gave him the pamphlets I told him that they were written in German and he couldn't read them.

Liberty War Bond, 1943. Bond cashed 1995, Uncle Sam only paid 35 years worth of interest total of $106.16.

He said, "Oh well, I just wanted to look at the pictures." Oh, yeah! I said. I found out later that he could read and speak German like an old pro.

Next day the front line was rather quiet in our sector. The Germans had started pulling back their forces into the foothills of the formidable Apennine Mountain range that housed the most destructive fortification (The Gothic Line) in Italian history. We were taking life rather easy when Sgt. McDermott decided to go out for a stroll. He came across shallow grave sites of two German soldiers (truck drivers) killed by our aircraft.

The local Italians had buried them in shallow graves by the roadside. He noticed a hand sticking out of the grave where the water erosion had washed away the soil, exposing the hand. On the hand was a ring or a watch (I am not sure which it was). Sgt. McDermott gently kicked it loose and took the article as another German collectable war Souvenir. WOW! What a guy! He loved combat and he collected German war souvenirs as collateral any time he killed or captured a German officer. He confiscated his pistol right then and there. That was the bounty that the officer had to pay.

I remember telling him one time, that the Germans would surely shoot him on the spot if ever captured with all that Germans loot hanging on him. He had a cool answer. He said to me, Pvt. Carroll, just remember this one thing, long as I have my rifle with plenty of ammo, I am not being captured. So why should I worry about it now! Do you understand partner? It's not going to happen. By the way it never did happen.

On another occasion, I remember when we captured a small village. A young German officer came out from under a pile of rubble and surrendered. Sgt. McDermott of course, asked him for his pistol.[4] The officer said he didn't have one, but Sgt. McDermott knew better. He hit him square on the chin, knocking him down. He then pointed to the direction of the rubble where the officer came from and said, "Go get the pistol or I will hit you again." The officer got the message. He got up brushed off his clothing, and away he went into the rubble and came out with the pistol.

Next day, orders came down to move out and be ready to outflank the city of Florence, by going farther over to the east. We were to go down to the Arno River, wade across in single file, and head north on Highway 65. That would take us straight into the Apennine Mountain range. I remember that evening very well. It rained cats and dogs all afternoon. We were soaking wet when we moved into a small farmhouse that had been prearranged for our use that afternoon.

We held up there just long enough for the issue of our new winter shoe-pacs (combat boots).[5] We changed out our footwear and were now ready to pull out on our next mission. The time was just right to test our new shoe-pacs, but our squad was in for a big surprise. When we stepped out of the house into total pitch darkness, everything went wrong. We began to slip and slide and fall like dominoes. We just couldn't stand up. Our traction wasn't just right in these new shoe-pacs. However, after a long struggle going down the slippery, muddy slopes of this dirt road, we began to walk on smoother ground and things got better. We began our march over to a new sector, closer to the Apennine Mountain range.

Chapter 4
BUILDING QUIVERED, SHOOK AND RATTLED

Later on that night we moved into a large, long, two-story building with a heavy tile roof that could withstand heavy mortar fire. It was a safe place to have a big poker game and then shortly thereafter, bed down for the night and enjoy some real pleasure time.

About 2100 hours we heard a heavy digging noise outside about 300 yards in front of us. Our officer got all excited about this noise and sent out a listening patrol to observe what was going on out there in no-man's land. The patrol came back very quickly and reported to our officer that about 30 Germans had dug in for the night. The only thing we could do was call in for heavy artillery fire to be lain in on the German position.

The artillery observer contacted and given the size of the enemy force and their combat readiness status. He immediately gave authorization to use five rounds of 155mm cannon fire. Word quickly came back from our cannoneers that five rounds would be on the way in about five minutes. Our building was right in the line of fire. Hopefully, the first round would hit its mark and not our building. "WOW," I said to Sgt. McDermott. The first shell might be short, then the next one would hit right in our hip pocket. What are we going to do about this?

He said, "Hell, I don't know. Just lay down flat on the floor and pray that the shells will go over our heads and hit the target."

Just a few moments later the shells came screaming right over our building, causing it to quiver, shake, and rattle. Although we were lying flat on the floor all shook up, we did have time to count our blessings as each projectile passed overhead. We had a mental count-down to the very last one. Then we all jumped up and let out a big yell, because we knew after that last shell passed over us that God had delivered us out of the hands of total destruction. If only one of those big projectiles had hit the side of the building, we certainly would have been totally wiped out.

Then we rejoiced. We were safe and very happy. The shells hit on target and disrupted the German garrison with no further action required from our company.

About 2400 hours that night, new orders came down for us to move out pronto. The orders directed our unit to move over to a new sector and set up a roadblock (called the crossroads) just a short distance from the Sieve River. The marching distance was approximately seven miles as the crow flies, and we had to be there before daylight. We got all packed up and stumbled out of that nice warm hotel bedroom (long barn) out into a very dark, dreary, night. We stood there wondering what could be worse than leaving this nice, warm place in the middle of the night.

Well, yes, things could be worse all right. We had no sooner gotten outside of the building when Germans began to lay in 88mm shells right on top of the building, causing us to take off in high gear. To complicate the problem even more, we ran into a reconnaissance combat team that had just run into a strong German combat patrol. The team had gotten all shot up.

This bad news caused our company to go on full alert through the rest of the trip. Since we had to scramble away from the heavy shelling on the building and go around the reconnaissance patrol team (a shot up mess), we become somewhat delayed. We force marched all night and got into the crossroads position before daylight.

Chapter 5
THE CROSSROADS AND BEYOND

The standing orders were to dig in and guard the crossroads until further orders. Just up the road to our right, at approximately 200 yards from our crossroads position, was a farmhouse previously used by the Germans for their command post. Right behind us on a small knoll our heavy weapons platoon dug in. Right above my head a water cooled, tripod heavy machine gun set-up to fire right down the main road leading into the foothills of the Gothic lines. The gunner was in his position set for a big firefight.

About 1100 hours that morning, we were all sitting around on the edge of our foxholes shooting the bull. Suddenly, two young German paratroopers, both 18 years of age, blond hair, and very nice looking chaps appeared right out in front of us. They stepped out of the heavy under-brush onto the main road, not more than a hundred yards down the road. They started walking up the road talking and laughing as they approached our position. They were dressed in full combat paratrooper uniforms with their little pot-shaped jump helmets strapped to their chins, and to our surprise, they were unarmed.

Our machine gunner saw them in plenty of time to adjust his tripod where he could fire directly on them, but evidently he panicked and froze in his position. Obviously, he fired too quickly. All the bullets went over their heads sparing their lives. The two paratroopers[6] hit the ground and crawled into the brush and began to call out, "Comrade, comrade." Meanwhile, Sgt. McDermott started walking toward them calling out for them to come out with both hands up. They came out of the brush nearly scared to death, shaking and trembling with both hands locked in place over their heads. He apprehended both and brought them back to the officer in charge for interrogation.

Later, we found out the reason why these two paratroopers were out mollycoddling around this time of day. They explained it this way to our officer. The house down the road to our right was their command post. They moved out the day before and moved farther up into the foothills of the Gothic lines. During their stay at this house they had met this young Italian maiden. She had served them some fine wine (vino) and they were going back for some more of that same stuff. Ho-Hum. What a soldier will do to get a small glass of vino!

After all the excitement was over, we began to settle down. We were all sitting around our foxholes eating our lunches of "K" rations, when I noticed this color-coded German telephone wire moving right in front of my fox-hole. I hollered out to Sgt. McDermott to come quickly and take a look at this telephone wire as it moved across the road right in front of my foxhole. Sgt. McDermott came running right over and took a big look as the end of the telephone wire moved into the brush. Sgt. McDermott said to me, "Catch hold of the wire and follow it out to the other end and you can capture an-other German. That will make three prisoners to send back to the rear." I said, "No thanks. I will let the Germans have the wire." By the way, the wire slipped right on through without my intervention.

The most significant thing about this wire wasn't that I didn't follow it out to the other end and capture the German, but the type wire it was! This wire was the latest state of the art, German technology used in the manufac-turing of this high quality macaroni vinyl plastic coated, color coded, Ger-man wire found no other place in the world. Only now is it being slowly replaced with the latest fiber optics technology.

Orders came down the next morning alerting us to be ready to move out. We broke camp around noontime and headed north crossing the Sieve River. Then we started our long trek into the formidable Apennine Mountain range where we bivouacked on the lower slope of Monticelli near the small village of Casacce. This area was a real hot spot. The Germans were laying in artil-lery and mortar fire thick and heavy. German 88s were screaming over head as well, and mortar shells were bursting all around us. This was the final leg of our treacherous journey up Hog-Back Ridge, to the summit of Monticelli Ridge.

I remember that evening while digging-in my foxhole. I looked over my shoulder and noticed a photographer trying to get pictures of a couple of other GIs and myself in his Universal Pictures News Reel Report. He wasn't having much luck. He finally stopped what he was doing and came over and asked us to look up more and keep on digging our foxholes. He wanted a good picture of the real GI digging-in under combat conditions while getting real dirt under his finger nails. We did just that and satisfied his request.

About two months later, I received a letter from home telling me that they had seen me on Newsreel at the local movie theater in Marietta, Okla-homa. This was quite a surprise for the home folks and a bigger surprise for me.

The sad part of that long awaited news story had finally arrived. These orders were directing Co. G to spearhead the final drive up the slope to the summit on Monticelli Ridge.

Before we pulled out that afternoon we got to observe our first big air-craft bombing run of the northern Italian campaign. Co. I moved up the ra-vine within about 400 yards of the summit on Monticelli Ridge when they ran into barb-wire entanglements and heavy machine gun and mortar fire, and began to suffer heavy casualties. After 25 men were wounded, the com-pany received orders to withdraw and set up a perimeter defense around I'Uomo Morto.

The enemy could look right down the throats of both companies, (I & K) and that's not where you want to be under these circumstances. That evening we were getting ready to pull out when we noticed a large flight of twin engine B-25 Mitchell bombers coming in and unloading their bombs in a heavy forested area. The bombs fell just a short distance up the slope a very short distance from Co. I and Co. K's dug in positions. The bombs exploded in the tall timber and made match stick size splinters out of the trees and changed the landscape in the area in a matter of seconds.

The first group of 25 bombers came in and dropped their bombs up the slope. Shortly thereafter, the second group came in and released its bombs in the same area. Whoa, what a loud thud! The explosion of the bombs sounded like all the bombs went off about the same time. It was what we call saturation bombing. The bombers made a quick turnaround and high tailed it back to their home base. From our view point, we were unable to determine if the bombs were hitting high enough upon the ridge to clobber the enemy or if they were hitting our own troops. (What we normally call friendly fire.) I guess we will never know. Anyway, friendly fire makes war casualties just like enemy fire. The individual Infantry soldier has to suffer regardless whose fire it is (friend or foe). We are expendable cannon fodder, you know!

Chapter 6
DAY ONE MONTICELLI RIDGE

The next day, 15 September 1944, the big shocker came down from Regimental Headquarters, stating that Co. G, 2nd Bn. 363rd Inf., would spearhead the main drive up the hog-back slope to the summit on Monticelli Ridge, the key position to the Gothic Line. Co. G moved out that afternoon, worming its way up the rugged slopes, crossing through deep ravines, rock crevices, and heavy underbrush along the timberline. Occasionally, we stopped for a 10 minute break.

After we moved through the timberline, we came out into the open meadow, the lower section of the summit, where we began to notice our first friendly comrades. They appeared to be a part of Co. B's light machine gun squad dug in along a five foot escarpment. We only waved at them and moved right on through their defensive position and went on up approximately a hundred yards or more toward the summit. Would you believe me? This is the very place we selected for our home for the next three days. Sgt. McDermott said to me, "It's getting dark.

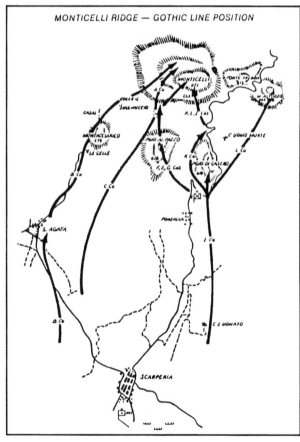

Monticelli Ridge – Gothic Line Position. Action of 363d Infantry, 12-18 Sept. 1944. Supported by 347 FA BN.

We need to dig-in and stabilize our position for the night."

About the time we started digging-in, here came Capt. Conley over to our squad, rather hurriedly. He ordered Sgt. McDermott to take his squad over to the left side of the ridge and set up a firing position to protect Co. G's left flank. We quit digging and moved over to the left flank and started digging-in once again. That's when we began to receive heavy sniper fire from our rear and bullets came so close to our ears that they sounded like firecrackers popping.

WHERE HAVE YOU BEEN BONNIE CARROLL? I CAN'T SHOOT THIS THING WITHOUT AMMO!

Sgt. McDermott spoke up right then and said, "Bonnie Carroll, looks like we are in for a big fight." Believe this story or not; the battle for Monticelli Ridge was the largest and most costly battle we fought during the whole Italian Campaign. Fortunately, we finished digging in that night without suffering any casualties. This was virgin territory, with no signs of 'Kilroy' ever being there.[7] Co. G was out there on the point right astride of the big, hogback ridge. There was no place to go but forward, spearheading the drive that would eventually break the German defenses on Monticelli Ridge, the key position to the Gothic line. Co. B was down the ridge below us over to our left. Henry Bowen and John Burklow, both of Co. E, my two trainee buddies, dug in over to my right, while Co. K was off to our right a short distance down the ridge.

Co. G's men were all cocked and primed to spearhead the all out attack on Monticelli Ridge. The attack clock was ticking and just when the alarm went off, Co. G was going up the ridge to the top of the summit on Monticelli Ridge.

Chapter 7
DAY TWO MONTICELLI RIDGE

I woke up very brightly and early the next morning (day two) and rose from my Sealy bed mattress and called up room service. Please send ham and eggs with melted cheese, and a hot cup of Maxwell House coffee, good to the last drop, and top it off with an assortment of fresh fruit. Oh yes, I forgot. One more thing, send a package of cigarettes and make them Lucky Strikes for my personal pleasure, please. After breakfast I walked out on the verandah to enjoy the azure blue sky above and the lush green valley that lay beyond on the valley floor below.

WOW! Lo and behold, I had just been woken up to the fact, that this event was not true, its only a dream. What I was really looking at was just a prelude to what was to come. I was looking straight down the barrel of the biggest artillery cannon in our arsenal. The 240mm Long Tom Cannon set poised and aimed right at us, ready to release the first salvo right into our position from the valley floor just outside of the town of Scarperia. I first saw a big flash followed by a big black puff of smoke. Immediately following this big puff came this large black ring of smoke, and out of that ring come this mosquito size object. As the object began to rise up, heading our way it became larger and larger. As the projectile got closer, and closer, it began to sound off like a freight train coming down the rail lines, full steam ahead.

Suddenly I realized that this monstrous shell was coming right at us, and I began to yell out, "Get down man, get down. This damned shell is going to hit right in the middle of us. Get

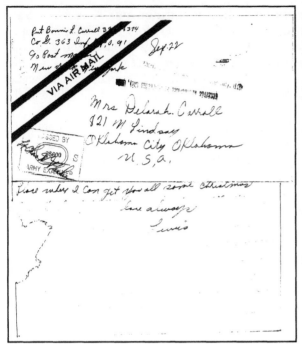

Letter written on stationery that was in Bonnie L. Carroll's backpack received a bullet hole through the outer edge of the paper on the second day of combat on Monticelli Ridge. Note: down in left hand corner of the envelope; all letters had to be read and examined by our Officer. This letter was examined by Lt. Flesher.

down. Wham-Bang-Blewee! It hit and exploded about 20 feet from my foxhole. Fortunately nobody was killed, but the concussion from this big dude was so strong that it pulled me up to the top of my foxhole and dropped me free fall to the bottom. Wham! This shook me up terribly. Then the loose dirt and rock (the small stuff) began to fall and nearly covered me over. A few seconds later the big stuff, (large clods of dirt and rock) began to fall from the sky like large hailstones.

This frightening close call became a big shocker for me, because I had previously selected this very spot to dig my foxhole. Obviously something just told me to move on up farther. I thought maybe the little bush that was out in front might draw enemy fire. I truly believe that the death angel[8] told my little ego sensor, "No not here," so I picked up my belongings and moved on up the slope a bit farther out of the impact zone. WOW! Otherwise, I'd blow into a million pieces. I feel like the Death Angel passed over me for the first time on Monticelli Ridge.

This was my first experience with "friendly fire." The only good thing that came out of this friendly fire bombardment was that we had a ready-made latrine about 20 feet wide and six feet deep. This shell hole gave us protection at night when mother nature called. We also used it as the authorized company trash dump. By the way, the other two shells went on over our heads and landed smack dab on the heavily fortified concrete bunker on the next hill over. The bunker housed the famous deadly accurate German 88mm artillery piece that was ripping our heavy truck traffic to pieces on the valley floor along the river Sieve.

The very next day a lone P-47 fighter bomber aircraft came over, and the pilot made a dive on the same bunker, dropping his bombs that finished knocking out the German 88.

Co. G became heavily engaged in combat throughout the daylight hours. Fighting off counterattacks coming from our left flank. Engaging in firefights with enemy snipers that penetrated our rear area. Sgt. McDermott, our one man army, was always ready for a big firefight to repel any counterattack, big or small, that came our way in the evenings about 6:00 p.m. He could always tell when the Germans were attacking. The first indication signal of an attack came from the German sergeant when he barked out the attack orders, or when the German sergeant blew his whistle to start the attack.

This was one of Sgt. McDermott's finest moments. He would call out, "Here they come, Get ready." Then he would pull off his helmet and crawl out of his foxhole to meet the charge. With his dead eye shooting ability he managed to stop all counterattacks before the Germans could get their attack rolling. After the first big counterattack was repulsed, I asked Sgt. McDermott why in the hell did he pull off his helmet and crawl out of his foxhole when the Germans made a counterattack. He said to me, "Bonnie Carroll, you've got to get out there where you can see the Germans coming and then put that

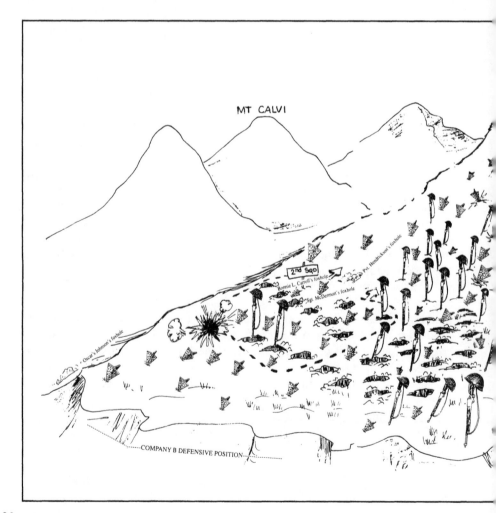

little red hole right through them before they do it to you. To do that you've got to keep your head down low and be able to see, and you certainly can't do that with this big pot helmet on your head. So I gently toss it off to do my home work."

After the morning counterattack had failed, the Germans began to infiltrate our rear area again. They got so close they began to toss hand grenades (potato mashers) into our foxholes. A buddy over to my left called out all excited and said, "Bonnie, did you hear that explosion?" I answered him right back saying I sure did!

"What happened to you?"

He said, "A German sniper slipped up and threw a potato masher right in my foxhole and it exploded!"

I said, "No kidding, are you hurt?"

He said, "No, but I had to scamper out of there like a gopher in a den of rattlesnakes and after it exploded I slid right back in like a scared rabbit. Whee, I sure out-smarted that German, didn't I?

ELLI RIDGE

SAM MOORE

I said, "You sure did, but be very careful and keep your head down and your brain working, because you know that German snipers are still out there and they are just waiting for a GI to stick his head up where they can take a crack at it."

Later on that evening that same sniper began to work on my foxhole. I noticed that the sniper was shooting at the gas chamber on my rifle, so I gently pulled it down into my foxhole. Later, a couple of shots rang out right over my position and I noticed that the sniper was shooting at my back pack that was lying just outside my foxhole. The only thing of value in it was my leather portfolio that I had just received from home the past week. The sniper put two holes through the pack and damaged my writing paper. I was able to salvage a couple of sheets out of the lot to get one letter off to my spouse just a couple of days after the great battle for Monticelli Ridge. She managed to keep all of my letters, including this special one, the only souvenir I have that came out of that great battle we fought on Monticelli Ridge.

Another sniper began to work on Sgt. McDermott's foxhole with sniper fire. He released a new weapon on Sgt. McDermott's position for the first time. It was a bright orange colored, hard plastic, rifle grenade, grooved to make it spend like a bullet for accuracy. It was a little larger than grandma's snuff box. The first grenade came in and hit just outside of his foxhole and exploded, sounding about as loud as a two inch firecracker.

A little later, another one came in and landed in the loose dirt just above his head and right at the edge of

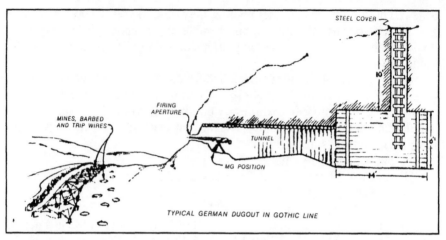

Heavy bunkered German machine gun positions like one in this sketch were located in strategic points overlooking Monticelli Ridge, making Company G the prime target for the initial assault.

his foxhole and it failed to explode. Sgt. McDermott reached up and pulled it in for his inspection and later on that evening passed it around for our evaluation. We thought at first the grenade was fired from a rifle launcher. However, afterwards, we came to the conclusion that it being launched from a flare pistol, which gave the German sniper a free hand to fire his rifle when he flushed Sgt. McDermott out of his foxhole.

However, that didn't happen, so Sgt. McDermott lived to fight another day. Sgt. McDermott came to a battlefield conclusion real quickly about this weapon. He said it was to lightweight and didn't carry enough destructive power to do much damage. He rated it higher on pure curiosity rather than a battlefield weapon.

Chapter 8
GERMAN OFFICER MADE A TRUCE PROPOSAL

A German officer and two soldiers came over the hill late in the afternoon on the second day during the battle for Monticelli Ridge. They were waving a white flag to offer a surrender proposal. One soldier was wounded. The other, about 17 years old, was apparently the officer's aide. The German officer met with our officer and after a short discussion and some hand waving, Sgt. McDermott went out to investigate. They finally broke off the negotiations and the three were taken as prisoners.

Sgt. McDermott returned to his foxhole and I asked him what the German officer wanted. He said that he wanted to give up his position only if we sent an officer and persons back with him to show good faith. He also wanted the two soldiers with him to come on over as prisoners because he had lost most of his men, the ones remaining either wounded and dying or starving to death. They hadn't had a bite to eat in over three days. That explanation sounded like a good, justifiable reason for the officer to give up his position, and a better reason for us to accept his surrender proposal. His proposals, however, were rejected.

Just before the prisoners moved away, Sgt. McDermott called out that a wounded GI soldier needed help off of the hill. The young German soldier came over to assist the wounded GI, Irwin Motner, off of Monticelli Ridge. They started their trek down the mountainside when the German soldier looked down and saw a small cracker on the ground discarded by a GI. He asked Motner if he could pick up the cracker to eat because he hadn't had anything to eat in over three days. Of course, Motner told him he could have it.

The remarkable thing about this conversation is that he spoke to him in the same German dialect that the young soldier was speaking. Man! This young German prisoner became really surprised! In fact, Motner was originally from Vienna, Austria, the same place the German was from, and he discovered that they had lived about five miles apart. The young 17-year-old German asked him how he got in the American Army. Motner only grinned and told him how he became drafted. You can imagine how that answer went over in the young German's mind. That statement coming from Motner surely confused him more than ever. I know Motner's life story so I will let you read on and find out for yourself.

We had taken 18 prisoners up until the time the German officer made his proposal. Because the officer brought with him a wounded soldier who was a German medic, and the 17 year old, and because they were all starving. I believe that the German officer was telling the truth. He became concerned about the welfare of his troops who were still alive. I think we made a mistake and should have accepted his offer. We should have sent an officer back with some troops to make them surrender.

Another thing that haunted me was our failure to attack at night. The Germans would attack our positions through the day and then pull back and bed down for the night inside of those big bunkers sheltered caves. The big question was why we didn't attack them at night while holed up inside those caves. I think we could have avoided the frontal assault up Monticelli Ridge where we got caught up in the crossfire that wiped out our company. I truly believe if we had done things differently that many lives would been saved. That's my opinion. What's yours?

Just below me, to my left looking down the ridge, two dead GIs lay dead killed the first morning of our encounter on Monticelli Ridge. Every time I looked out of my foxhole the next two days, I would see these two GIs lying there dead as a doornail. It gave me a queasy feeling because they lay there in two shallow foxholes that offered no protection whatsoever. The two GIs had been possibly easy pickings for German snipers that were roaming around in our rear area looking for easy prey. Near hits from mortar fire have wiped out GIs in real shallow foxholes before, and why these two experienced GIs didn't take note of past experiences and dig deeper was a mystery to me. God only knows.

Pvt. Roberts, my new combat buddy from Oklahoma, had just come on line a couple of weeks before. He had just received his new stainless steel trench knife with beautiful handles with scabbard to match that his dad had made him for his birthday. He was really proud of his new knife. In fact I liked it, also, and mentioned to Sgt. McDermott that I'd really like to have one like that for myself.

About noontime, Pvt. Roberts raised his head up trying to locate a sniper that was just a short distance behind us down the ridge line. When he raised up the last time, the sniper shot him through the front part of his mouth and the bullet came out through the back part of his neck, seriously wounding him. He managed to survive the initial impact and he lay in his foxhole for a couple of hours without going into shock. Meanwhile, we managed to talk to him and persuaded him to stay calm and cool. Eventually, he began to panic and was crying out for help. He said he was bleeding to death. Unfortunately, there were no medic's in the area to help him.

All of us were pinned down and we knew for sure if we stuck our heads up, we would also get shot. The chances would be even greater if we had gotten out of our foxholes to try to help him. We pleaded with him to stay down for at least two more hours and we would get him out under the cover of darkness. I really felt sorry for him, because I couldn't help him under the existing circumstances. There were buddies much closer to him than I was, and they couldn't get to him either.

Finally he made his last call for help and cried out, saying, "I'm bleeding to death. I can't wait any longer. I'm getting out of here right now. I have got to get help." He crawled out of his foxhole, stood up and started down the hill when the sniper opened fire and shot him once again; he fell dead just a few feet from his foxhole.

Approximately 10:00 hours the next morning I heard our BAR (Browning Automatic Rifle) open up and seven shots rang out. "WOW, what was that?" I said. This was an unusual event, our BAR didn't open up unless something unusual is happening. Heads began to pop up all over the place and a lot of excited GIs began to ask, "What happened? What happened?"

When we found out later that afternoon, Pvt. Hendrickson, our BAR man, had just put seven red holes through a German sniper. The sniper came over the top of the ridge and had slipped into Pvt. Hendrickson position. The German sniper was charging Pvt. Hendrickson with a potato masher, already fused, and he was in the forward throwing motion when Pvt. Hendrickson looked up and saw the sniper at his front door. WOW, what a close call! Pvt. Hendrickson grabbed his BAR and let loose with seven rounds just in time to save his day. The German sniper fell forward dead, and the potato masher exploded just short of Pvt. Hendrickson's foxhole, without inflicting any damage to him.

That night, after the regular evening German counterattack had been repulsed, we all had to slip over and take a good look at this German suicide attempt, because he was the first German sniper that had ever penetrated our position from a frontal assault and gotten this close. Others tried it many times from our left flank, but they, too, were repelled with heavy losses. The snipers that slipped around our lower left flank and came up behind us roaming the area at free will dealt us the most misery.

Chapter 9
DAY THREE ON MONTICELLI RIDGE

We received our new 2nd lieutenant[9] (replacement) fresh from the good old USA. He was a small person and very friendly type of a guy. The first night on the ridge he made his round to see every GI in his foxhole, talking to everybody individually. He asked a lot of questions about our personal needs. He asked me how I thought the battle was going and I told him I thought the battle was going in our favor, since we had taken six or eight prisoners already the first day. He went on to say that he had just received a letter from home and his spouse had just given birth to their first child. He was really proud of being a father, a real dad to a baby girl.

Before he moved over to the next GIs foxhole, I just had to tell him that I was the official poker card deck carrier for the squad. I would set up a big poker game for us tomorrow night. I told him I would do it just when the mortar barrage, sniper fire, and the regular evening counterattack diminished. He said to count him in. I said, "Okay sir, you're in. I'll send word around when I get everything in place."

The next day orders came down for Co. G to make the frontal assault, rifle charge up the hog-back slope to the summit on Monticelli Ridge. Our new lieutenant called out the order to make the charge. He was one of the first persons out of his foxhole charging up the slope, when a German machine gunner opened up on him with a murderous crossfire of machine gun bullets that cut him to pieces. The same machine gunfire riddled the rest of the company as they charged up the slope.

Over to my right was this GI from Chicago, Illinois. He was probably in his early 30s, married and had two young girls. He had just received his "Dear John" letter from home and was rather shaken up and disturbed about his wife's love affair. She was asking him for a divorce. He said she had found another love. He evidently didn't care if he lived or died, because of the way he acted when he made that big charge up the slope when orders came down to attack.

He stormed out of his foxhole and got cut down by heavy machine gunfire. He fell to his knees and just gritted his teeth and said, "You SOB; I'm coming after you. He raised up and lunged forward again, but only to get a few feet farther when the machine gunner cut him down for the second time. He slumped forward and fell dead just a few feet outside his doorstep (foxhole).

The battle for Monticelli Ridge was still raging in fervor. Capt. Conley[10] was looking for officers to command and Pfc. Oscar Johnson, Co. B was crawling around looking for guns and ammo. Meanwhile, Sgt. McDermott, Pvt. Bonnie L. Carroll, Pvt. Hendrickson, our BAR man, and Sgt. Hubbard, squad leader from another platoon, and one other BAR man from another squad were the only men left alive. We were out on the point, on the left flank of the ridge, pinned down, and stuck out like a sore thumb, facing the whole German Army with no place to go.

Sgt. McDermott was firing away at the oncoming Germans, firing right over my foxhole. He said he stopped the counterattacks before they could muster any force and then started firing into the machine gunner's position who was providing the overhead fire support for the attacking Germans. Sgt. McDermott further substantiated his action by saying his eye caught the trajectory of the German machine gunner's tracer bullets that were marking him as a target. The fiery bullet was exposing the enemy's machine gun position as well.

Sgt. McDermott took advantage of the situation. As the fire spitting bullets whizzed by his head, his sharp eye followed them right back to the enemy position about five hundred yards out. He then directed his own rifle fire right into the enemy's position putting it out of action.

I know one thing, without a doubt in my mind, if it hadn't been for Sgt. McDermott's non-wavering bravery and superb marksmanship, the Germans would have over-run our position time after time and completely wiped us out. We were the stop-gap squad for our company. Only eight GIs plus Capt. Conley escaped this onslaught of 142 men, and only by the grace of God we walked off of Monticelli Ridge alive. Everybody else was either killed or wounded and evacuated.

For me to tell the real story and get Capt. Conley or anybody else to listen would be a significant fact. The story has to receive more attention from higher authority. Not from a little private GI, like me, to verify Sgt. McDermott's story. I think he should have received a high honor for his action on Monticelli Ridge. He won the battle but lost the glory. He went on to win two silver stars for his valor, which gives you some idea what a great soldier he really was.

To further verify who was the lead company spear-heading the drive up Monticelli Ridge, let's look at the casualty list and then find out who lost the most men on the initial charge. Then you will see for yourself. If any other company was astride that big, hog-back ridge like we were, they are bound to have a better story than what I have been able to tell thus far.

The attack cost Co. E, seven killed and 27 wounded. It cost Co. G, (during the first five minutes) 25 killed and 32 wounded. Total losses for three days fighting, 36 killed and 92 wounded. Co. B lost 14 killed and 126 wounded, a remarkably low kill rate of 14 against (undisclosed number wounded). I have no record of how many men Co. K lost in the initial attack. If the death lists were even close or greater than Co. G's casualty list, I am sure somebody will have something to say about it.

After the battle of Monticelli Ridge was over with, Sgt. McDermott came over to my foxhole and talked to me about Pvt. Roberts' knife. He said,

"Bonnie Carroll, go over and take that knife[11] that you liked so well off of Pvt. Roberts body and use it for yourself. I am sure that Pvt. Roberts would like for you to have it.

I said "Yeah, but I can't take that knife from his dead body." I also realized that the knife would probably wind up in the non-personal pile of belongings, and never get back to his family. Nevertheless, I just couldn't take it, Period.

The battle for Monticelli Ridge had subsided; the rolling thunder of cannon fire had moved on to the next mountain range; the survivors of this terrible slaughter brought together (eight GIs & Capt. Conley). He assembled us to give us our last rites (blessings), which was our new assignment.

Chapter 10
HONOR THE DEAD

Meanwhile, Capt. Conley advised us that we must take a head count of the dead before we left the ridge. To do this we had to walk among the dead and fix bayonets on each dead man's rifle. Then stick the rifle in the ground with his helmet placed on the butt end to mark the exact location of each fallen hero. After this was accomplished, we came back together and tallied up the count, and made the official count of 36 dead. I thought this was a very patriotic way to honor our dead and mark the exact location of each fallen hero. It was very sad and a touching moment for me, also. I had become very close to some of these GIs. After the official count was made, Capt. Conley advised us to relax. We would remain on Monticelli Ridge that night and wait for further orders.

Next morning, 18 September 1944, we received our new orders and started trotting off the ridge in single file for the last time. We moved along the ridge line to the right of the summit. We started our downward decent down to the road on the backside of the mountain. I looked back to pay my last respect to our buddies, our fallen Heroes, and this was what I observed. I saw dead men scattered all over this hog-back ridge, all the way up near the summit. They looked like fallen leaves. These dead men lay in silent sleep beside their rifle markers that we had erected in their honor the evening before.

John Burklow, my friend and combat buddy died on Monticelli Ridge. He is buried in the US Military Cemetery, Florence, Italy.

Battle Casualty List

CASUALTIES
4 July 1944 - 30 April 1945

	MIA	KIA	DOW	SWA	LWA	INJ	TOTAL	RTD
Reg. Hq. Co.	0	4	0	4	12	1	21	9
Service Co.	0	0	0	1	6	1	8	5
Antitank Co.	0	1	1	6	7	6	21	12
Canon Co.	0	3	0	7	10	4	24	15
Medical Det.	2	22	1	24	43	12	104	43
Hq. Co., 1st Bat	0	5	0	6	13	3	27	12
A Co.	0	36	4	45	97	14	196	104
B Co.	1	49	6	39	93	13	201	83
C Co.	0	33	8	51	89	11	192	55
D Co.	0	1	3	7	25	5	41	23
Hq. Co., 2nd Bat	0	2	2	10	8	0	22	9
E Co.	0	30	2	51	101	5	189	84
F Co.	6	29	3	49	88	10	185	84
G Co.	1	55	3	60	104	10	233	71
H Co.	0	4	1	8	5	3	21	10
Hq. Co., 3rd Bat	0	5	0	3	15	5	28	14
I Co.	17	57	3	48	94	17	236	79
K Co.	2	39	3	45	108	11	208	76
L Co.	13	62	6	35	123	17	256	95
M Co.	0	6	0	8	16	2	32	13
TOTAL	**42**	**443**	**46**	**507**	**1057**	**150**	**2245**	**896**

BATTALION CASUALTIES
4 July 1944 - 30 April 1945

	MIA	KIA	DOW	SWA	LWA	INJ	TOTAL	RTD
Seperate Cos.	2	30	2	42	78	24	178	84
1st Bn.	1	124	21	148	317	46	657	277
2d Bn.	7	120	11	178	306	28	650	258
3d Bn.	32	169	12	139	356	52	760	277
TOTAL	**42**	**443**	**46**	**507**	**1057**	**150**	**2245**	**896**

MIA - Missing in Action   SWA - Seriously Wounded in Action
KIA - Killed in Action   LWA - Lightly Wounded in Action
DOW - Died of Wounds   INJ - Injured
RTD - Returned to Duty

Looking back down the ridge from the right side of the summit, I saw the horrors and destruction of war everywhere. German mortar tail fins that guided the main body of the little bomb right on target. Hundreds of them were standing upright in the middle of a small pothole, blackened by the explosive power of these powerful little mortars. Each one looked as though it was planted there by hand, which set the stage for this panoramic view of this great battlefield.

The morning dew began to settle on these hundreds of tail fins forming small droplets of water. As the morning sun began to creep over the horizon, the bright sun began to reflect off of these tiny droplets, sending out twinkling glitter of light rays that danced across the battlefield. It looked like a fairy wonderland. Looking even closer at these fins, hundreds of them standing there. They reminded me of a field of ripened pineapples with their spiny leaves protruding upward as though they were reaching skyward to fetch a drink of the morning dew.

This was truly a beautiful sight that only God could lay out so magnificently among our fallen heroes. This signified to me that God's power, glory, and heavenly splendor will last forever. This was truly a phenomenon for me to remember forever.

A cool breeze, THE WIND OF GLORY, was blowing across the meadow slopes that morning and the only movement I could see was the bent blades of grasses leaning my way. For the last time, as our battered Co. "G" was leaving our fallen buddies lying there in silent sleep, I heard a little whisper in the wind blowing across my ear saying, "So long buddies. Powder River Let'er Buck (the 91st Inf.'s battle cry).

Chapter 11
BACKSIDE OF MONTICELLI RIDGE

As we moved on farther down and around the left side of the ridge, I looked down into the deep ravine and saw this lone dead GI lying on the ground in spread eagle fashion. The body was right next to a German barb wire entanglement and heavy fortified positions. A German mortar shell had come in and landed about one foot from his head. Apparently he had dodged the first mortar; but, the second one got him, blowing away his helmet and taking off the whole top of his head. Evidently, the rest of the squad escaped without harm and continued the attack up the ravine to assist in breaking the backbone of this formidable German Gothic line of defense.

We moved on down to the main road on the backside of Monticelli Ridge and started going through heavy timber when I noticed this large German truck. The truck, loaded with black bread, bombed by our aircraft and thrown up on the hillside with all the bread intact. It had been raining that morning and the bread was beginning to ferment and swell up over the top of the truck's six-foot high sideboards. However, the bread was still pretty fresh and was throwing off a strong fresh bread aroma. It really sharpened our appetite for fresh bread; nevertheless, we had to keep right on moving. A little later a group of German prisoners came marching by and they smelled the fresh bread, also. I knew they must have been hungry, because this was their bread ration for the past two weeks. However, they had to march right on by without any bread for their hungry stomachs as we did.

We moved on down the highway for a couple of miles and entered a heavily forested area and dug in for the night, awaiting new orders and our new replacements. Next morning bright and early, we received our replacements, with orders to move out and head north. We were to catch up with our runaway division that had lunged forward after the big break through that left us far behind. Our company becomes devastated; we didn't have enough spunk left in our bones to chase after anybody.

As we moved out that morning, I began to notice all of the dead German Soldiers lying alongside the roadway. Many were upon the highway, and others were out in the open field, strung out for at least a quarter of a mile. These German Soldiers fully dressed for combat readiness and well dispersed in single file moving up for front line combat duty. They showed no signs of a struggle. I didn't really notice any heavy road bombardment from our artillery or aircraft. So what was the mystery behind this massacre? Obviously, they were being rushed into the front lines as a stop gap force with orders to move in at all cost. These troops evidently got caught up in our attacking forces, and were overwhelmed. They become mowed down like flies before they realized that we had broken through their lines running rampant. When Co. "G" came upon this big turkey shoot, it was a nasty mess. It was a massacre in the worst way.

When our heavy truck traffic began to roll north, you just couldn't imagine what had happened to these German soldiers that were lying on the surface of the road. Nobody took the time to remove them. I saw whole German soldier bodies mashed flat as a cookie sheet, body parts, heads, legs, arms, etc. you name them; they were all smashed "flat as a flitter." Whatever body part flattened on the pavement depended strictly on the soldier's position when he fell across the highway. Yes, this was a very nasty site, all right, but this was war, you know!

Approximately a week later, there was a survey team who came by our unit. They wanted somebody that was in the battle on Monticelli Ridge who was familiar with the battlefield and the terrain etc. They wanted him to go back with them to help look for the dead and make a record of the battle that took place there. Platoon Sgt. Kenneth Hubbard was selected out of our platoon and went back with them and this was what he observed and reported back to our company. He said the Germans had caves dug out on the backside of Monticelli Ridge that would house and feed a company of men. There was a complete field kitchen and a cave large enough to stable and feed 20 pack mules.

Outside the caves they found approximately 100 dead German soldiers lying along the perimeter of the ridge line. Apparently, they were trying to get organized to make a counterattack when our overwhelming artillery fire caught up with them and wiped them out.

The battle line moved on north and Co. "G" was getting ready to go back on the front line in the next few days for more heavy combat action. We stayed off just long enough to receive our new replacements, lick our wounds, cool our nerves, and then back to the front we went.

Chapter 12
THE FORGOTTEN FRONT

During the Gothic Line, Apennine Po Valley Campaign, the 5th Army received very little publicity; although, during this period (September through November 1944) the 5th Army lost 500 men per mile of territory gained. That's more losses than any other combat unit in the European Theater.

The valiant attack on Monticelli Ridge, 16 September 1944, cost Co. G, 25 dead and 32 wounded the first five minutes of the attack. Total loss for three days fighting, 36 dead, 92 wounded.

The 5th Army received three Bronze Stars for the Northern Italian Campaign. In France many divisions rode across France, Belgium, and Germany hardly fired a shot and received seven Bronze Battle Stars for their achievements. This was also true in Italy, when the 10th Mountain Div. came on line near the end of the war. They had a few skirmishes with the Germans, and afterwards tried to lead us to believe that they had won the war in northern Italy. No doubt, they were a well trained fighting force, but they lacked the combat experience that the 5th Army's old combat divisions had already mustered.

The new 10th Mountain Div. came into combat full of "piss and vinegar," because of all of that fine publicity they received while training back in the States. They trained purposely for mountain fighting. We didn't; we had to learn the hard way, from brute gut strength, blood, sweat, and tears.

Chapter 13
FUTA PASS AND BEYOND

Futa Pass, a key position to the Gothic Line that was over to our right on Highway 65, taken by our combat buddies of the 362nd Inf. Reg. We were attacking the Germans along the foothills straight ahead of us when we came upon a river deep below us worming its way through a long narrow green valley. Looking further ahead, we could see two large mountain peaks that indicated to us that the fighting ahead of us was going to be really tough. Orders had just come down for us to hold up and dig in for the night. We had reached our objective for the day.

WOW! Guess what? We were being fed hot chow! The chow wagon was on its way up and we were to have a big hot meal right out of those big fancy containers. This hot food delivered up front was a special treat, man, because it didn't happen every day on the front lines. In addition to the chow wagon bringing us mess kits, it also provided hot water furnaces to scald our eating utensils before and after we ate our gourmet food. Oh yes, I almost forgot, much to our delight they also brought along toilet paper. We not only used it for the intended purpose but also used to wipe our hands.

To make our day complete we decided to have a big poker game (Infantry soldiers' pastime). We had just been paid and our pockets were bulging with fresh money (allied issued money). All we needed was time to spend our play money for something worthwhile. We laid out a shelter halve and seated ourselves around our makeshift gambling table and started betting with old beat up poker cards that I had been carrying in my shirt pocket for months. I'm sure the cards were just waiting for the day for use one more time in a big poker game. No sooner had we started betting when the chow wagon appeared, disrupting our poker game.

Chow time called and away we went to grab our mess kit and fall in line for chow. No sooner had we gotten in line for chow when, whiz bang (grizzz-sizzz), a German 88 shell came in and hit a haystack. The haystack was located off to our right rear about 20 yards from where we lined up for chow. The haystack was blown into a million pieces and GIs scattered like quail. Unfortunately, I was the only one who had dug a foxhole, and you can bet on one thing, I had a house full of company. Four GIs came running over to my foxhole, and they all tried to jump in at the same time, but they just didn't fit. Luckily, that was the only shell that came in, so we began to settle down and get ready for our evening chow. The chow servers called on one chow hound (GI) to come through the chow line at a time.

Before the afternoon was over we were lucky. We got to observe a little sideshow for a change. We noticed a P-47 aircraft come over us real low. It made a sharp left turn, went into a steep dive down into the valley, and released a big bomb on a farmhouse across the river, the house being located approximately a thousand yards away from our position. The bomb hit close enough to shake up the occupants inside the house, but the house wasn't destroyed. The P-47 came back up, circled, and went back in for the kill. Meanwhile, we noticed two Germans run out of the house. They jumped on their motorcycle and took off down the dirt road, speeding hell bent for leather. They were headed down the road, trying to make a clean get away, when the aircraft opened up on them with all guns blazing.

You should have seen how those two Germans crashed that motorcycle and hit the dirt. They dove into a big bar-ditch for cover while the aircraft made another circle overhead and came back in again for the kill. We were unable to determine the outcome of that event. However, I bet those two Germans had their pants scared off of them if they were lucky enough to escape the aircraft's machine gunfire. What do you think?

Next morning, orders came down for us to move out and cross the river and go into a reserve holding position about a thousand yards from the river. We dug in that evening for the night and were sitting on the edge of our foxholes, shooting the usual GI bull. All of a sudden we heard a loud yell coming from our rear, approximately 500 yards up the slope in a heavy brush area. A German was yelling for help and waving a white flag. We dropped everything and got a litter team together and headed up there to find out what was wrong.

The German soldier stayed behind to take care of his seriously wounded comrade who received a bullet wound through the upper portion of his right leg. His leg had swollen terribly and gangrene had already set in. Our medic's gave him three vials of morphine to put him to sleep. I don't know if that was enough to put him to sleep forever or not, but he certainly went to sleep in a hurry.

Newsbreak: Just before dark one of our new replacements accidentally shot himself in the foot. Could this have been accidental or self-inflicted? Who knows? Accidents do happen you know.

Chapter 14
BOUNCING BETTY BOOBY TRAP

Our company moved over near the town of Rifredo and began attacking Poggio-Pioto in conjunction with the 338th Tank Inf. attack on Firenzola. By early afternoon Co. E had one squad on Pioto. Co. G was pushing in hot pursuit of the enemy around the base of the ridge on toward our next objective. Our main objective was a large stone house that sat back in a large clump of tall chestnut trees. I noticed that the trees were loaded with ripe chestnuts just about ready to drop. The month of October was just around the corner and in northern Italy, that's the beginning of the fall and winter season. The weather was already beginning to cool things down. A lot of drizzling rain and heavy fog moved in to make life terribly miserable for GIs living in foxholes day in and day out.

Co. G was advancing single file down a rocky road at a fast pace when the lead squad came upon a large, spring-fed water fountain. The fountain being built right into the side of a rock wall near the road. The local people came here from the big house just a short distance down the road to wash their clothes and water their cattle. The fountain made an ideal place for Co. G to stop and fill up.

The lead platoon broke rank, and went over to the fountain and drank and filled up their canteens to the brim. They moved on up the road to make room for the other squads to come in and fill up. The first scout of the first platoon moved on up the road about 30 feet ahead of the other troops. When he did he tripped on a booby-trap wire that released a Bouncing Betty Mine that jumped up in the air about 20 feet high and exploded, releasing hundreds of ball bearing size slugs.

The first blast we heard from afar become muffled. Then a few seconds later, another big vibrant blast was heard. It sounded like a small bomb went off. Whoa! What was that loud explosion I heard up front? Send word up and find out something! You men. There is something wrong up there. Word finally came back down the line telling us that the first scout of the first platoon had tripped on a booby trap wire that released a Bouncing Betty, an anti-personnel bomb.

Is it hard for you to believe this story? Evidently, the blast zone was too high and all of the slugs went straight out over the heads of the first squad. Instead of raining death and destruction down on the squad like the bomb was supposed to have worked. Evidently the bomb's malfunction saved our day. Not one single slug found its mark.

Our company filled up with fresh, sweet, spring water and went on our merry, happy way, looking for a firefight over on the next hill.

Chapter 15
MONTECATINI REST CENTER

Co. G had just spent seven days of glory at Montecatini 5th Army rest center. This was a city of hotels and hot baths, clean clothes, and good food. Then we were off again to the front lines to do more of the same: attack and attack. While at Montecatini, we found the rooms were cold with no heat. We slept on army cots with only one blanket under us and one to cover with. The second night we gathered up every Stars and Stripes newspaper found and put them underneath the blankets we slept on to help keep out the bitter cold. Another unusual thing was that the toilets found stopped up and wouldn't work; so we had to use outside slit trenches when mother nature called.

Gosh! After living in those dirty foxholes for five weeks on the front lines, eating K-rations and pulling 100% alert duty, this place was like living in paradise. The only bad part about this pleasure time was it ran out too quickly. Just think, after seven days at Montecatini we were on our way back to that dreadful front line and began to endure the terrible hardships all over again.

God only knows what kind of a sector we would get this time. Some sectors were hot and others were rather quiet. It depended a whole lot on the type of real estate the Germans were defending, of course. If it were important to them you can bet your bottom dollar that the sector would be hot. They would defend an important position to the last man. The Germans were always ready to pick a firefight for the high ground along this heavy traveled highway. Sometimes the encounter was so close that we could hear them breathing and certainly smell them. Whoa, I bet they could smell us too!

Our truck convoy was approaching the battered town of Monghidoro, when we noticed up ahead that the lead truck turned left onto a dirt road and began to travel down toward a large farm house. It gave us a strong indication that we were going in the same direction. When we got to the turn-off, our truck made the same turn and went further down the dirt road about two more miles. We stopped, unloaded and went into bivouac for the night. Next morning we had a quick breakfast, broke camp and fell out in combat readiness waiting for our new orders, our attack plan. We had just received our 13 replacements, so we were up to full combat strength.

They issued us full field rations, three boxes of K-rations, with two extra bandoleers of ammunition making us ready for battle. These field rations meant we would be attacking the enemy all day long without let up until we accomplished our assigned mission. Capture, our objective. No hot meals, no dry socks, no nothing! We would be totally on our own.

The 2nd Platoon moved into position that morning and then we were ready to attack the enemy full blower ahead. This is combat! You're ready to make the sacrifice. For me this was like being on death row. The only difference up front you never know when or where your time might come. It was always a mystery for me to worry about just when that time might come! I was always hoping it wouldn't happen to me. However, you don't have many choices. You have to take some chances while under enemy fire. Don't you think? That's my opinion. What's yours?

Chapter 16
VICINITY OF CADEL TOSCO

Our company moved into the vicinity of Cadel Tosco and started advancing over the next hill when we came upon a farm house that Capt. Conley selected for his command post. We pushed on out and established a defense line and dug in for the night. Meanwhile, word came down that our platoon sergeant (Cvitjanovich) had received his field commission, making him a 2nd lieutenant.

Capt. Conley was going to have a special ceremony tomorrow afternoon, honoring him by hanging a set of gold bars on his shoulders, making him our first field commissioned officer. Capt. Conley told Sgt. McDermott to send out a couple squads of men and set up a defense line along the perimeter of that wooded section up the draw. "Go approximately 100 yards out to our right and provide protection while the ceremony was going on," he said.

Our 2nd Squad, started up the draw and ran into machine gun and mortar fire a short distance up the draw. Our new replacement officer, Lt. John McKay, brought us to a halt and ordered us to the rear. Later the 3rd Squad moved up the draw and started across the open field toward the wooded sector when a machine gunner opened up on them, pinning them down. The exchange of small arm's fire went on for 15 minutes or more but the 3rd Squad could not dislodge the machine gunner. Sgt. McDermott sent a messenger up the draw to find out what had happened and if they needed help. The squad leader sent word back that the squad was all right; no casualties suffered so far. "Just give us a little more time," he said, "and we will work our way out of this mess."

The ceremony was over and the new lieutenant came walking out of the house with a big smile on his face, ready for battle, while taking on a new mission. He asked Sgt. McDermott about the trouble that the 3rd Squad was having up the draw. Sgt. McDermott told him that the machine gunner was squeezing off his shots, one at a time, making it very difficult for the men to locate him. Sgt. McDermott went on to say that the squad wasn't in real serious trouble and would be back in a short while. Obviously, the new lieutenant didn't see it that way. He saw it differently. He told Sgt. McDermott to give him a gun and three good men and he would go up and relieve the squad.

Lt. Cvitjanovich grabbed a rifle and the three men hurried off up the draw where he made contact with the squad leader. He told him to start withdrawing his men because he was taking over. The withdrawal procedure was implemented and the squad got out safely. The day began to drag on into the late afternoon and the exchange of small arm's fire had stopped. Sgt. McDermott said to me, "We better go up there and see about the lieutenant. He could be in a bunch of trouble because we haven't heard an exchange of gunfire in over 30 minutes."

Our squad went on full alert, combat readiness. Meanwhile, Sgt. McDermott had talked to Sgt. Homer Weeden, 4th Platoon, about our weapons platoon, about mortar fire support during the attack on the Germans position. Okay, everything was set for the attack.

On our way up the draw, we ran into Sgt. Hiatt who told Sgt. McDermott he knew exactly the location of the German operating position. So we stopped and dug a firing pit for Sgt. Weeden to take cover in while he was laying mortar fire on the Germans' position.

Sgt. Weeden released all of the mortar shells on the enemy's position and shortly thereafter joined us as we moved up the draw. As we got near the open field, we heard a burst of machine gunfire and then everything became quiet. We continued our advance up a small ditch that led us up to where the lieutenant was lying all sprawled out. As we approached the scene, we knew something was seriously wrong, because his helmet was off his head and laying to one side.

Sgt. McDermott crawled up to where he was lying and looked at his face and saw that the sniper had shot him through the head. He died instantly. Sgt. McDermott pulled back and organized the squad in preparation for attacking the machine gun position, but after he analyzed the situation, he decided that the gunner had pulled out.

This was one time I noticed that Sgt. McDermott was really all shook up over the loss of Lt. Cvitjanovich. In fact, in all the battles we had been in and the many buddies we had lost, this loss was the one that pushed Sgt. McDermott over the brink. He actually showed his emotions this time. He ranted and raved, on and on, about the death of Lt. Cvitjanovich. He said he was going to kill every German machine gunner he saw from now on, even up to the very end of the war. Eventually Sgt. McDermott cooled himself down and began to act like himself once again. He started doing the same thing he always did best; that is, picking off Germans one at a time. However, he would wipe out larger groups when he caught them inside a big bunker.

Lt. Cvitjanovich, no doubt, was an outstanding soldier. Losing him was a great loss to our platoon and company. We definitely missed him, but Sgt. McDermott took over the job, temporarily, for a short time until we could get a replacement, and he did a great job. For the short time I knew Lt. Cvitjanovich, I would have given him very high marks for being a very brave soldier. I had noticed him once before when we made a frontal attack on a farmhouse. The house we assaulted was located in a wooded section where we had to cross a deep draw to reach our objective.

Just before the jump-off, we begin to receive heavy sniper fire from the house. I noticed then (Sgt.) Cvitjanovich being out of his foxhole looking over the area where the sniper fire was coming from. Bullets were whizzing right by his head and he just ducked down a little bit and went right on doing his business as usual. We could see smoke coming out of the chimney when we attacked the house later on that afternoon. The Italian family living in the house was found safely inside the house. The two Germans that ran out the back door when Sgt. Cvitjanovich flushed them out ran for the barn and were shot by Sgt. McDermott while trying to get away.

Chapter 17
ATTACK ON HILL 863 CA DA CARDINO

The attack on Ca Da Cardino Hill 863 cost our platoon six casualties. I remember very vividly when we received our six replacements and attacked Ca Da Cardino. By the end of the day all of the replacements were gone, either wounded, killed or just disappeared. The big question was always the same. "Why did these new replacements get hit or killed and the old hands seemed to survive the rigorous life of combat duty on the front lines?" God only knows. Maybe it was just plain luck and lots of combat experience. You know that I am only guessing. That's my opinion. What's yours?

Sgt. McDermott's 2nd Squad started the attack up Hill 863 toward the outskirts of this small village, when we began to receive heavy machine gunfire from the window of a house. The gunner had us pinned down and was dealing us lots of misery by wounding a couple of our men. Meanwhile Sgt. McDermott was working his way around the high ground where he could see him better while we fired into the gunner's position to get his attention. Bang! The gunner was dead. As we entered the outskirts of the village we began to receive heavy mortar fire. Man, the Germans laid mortar fire in on us thick and heavy. Luckily we made it through the mortar barrage with the loss of only two men wounded and then we entered the village continuing our attack.

Sgt. Hiatt went around the other side of the house and flushed out a German officer who came around the house meeting Sgt. McDermott head on. When Sgt. McDermott hollered out to him "Halt," he didn't, and it cost him his life. As our squad moved into the village, two more Germans flushed out and Sgt. McDermott shot them as they ran out the back way. Another one stuck his head out from behind a wall and he shot him between the eyes. Making a total of five enemies killed for the day. Next day our squad moved on toward Montepiano, when we hit a German machine gunner that's left behind to slow up our drive and to serve as a delaying action force. Poor guy, he didn't have a chance, sitting out by himself like that. He should have held his fire and given up. He would have lived longer. It only took one shot from deadeye McDermott's rifle to end that episode.

Chapter 18
BATTLE FOR MONTEPIANO

The battle for Montepiano was a stiff fight for our company, but we managed to capture it before dark. In doing so, we bottled up some more prisoners, and as always I was the lucky one to take them back to the command post. The battle for the town, in the vicinity of Montepiano, cost our company five casualties. On my way back from the command post I ran into two wounded GIs that were walking back to the aid station. One of them shot through both jaws and had a big bandage wrapped around his chin and up and over the top of his head. The wound was probably wrapped this way to keep his jaw in place. I imagine he had some teeth shattered also, but he seemed to be in good spirits and wasn't hurting too badly.

The other GI was carrying his helmet in his arm and I asked him what was wrong. He said that he got shot through his helmet and received a wound in the back of his neck. That seemed strange and I asked him how it happened. He showed me his helmet and sure enough it had a bullet hole right through the top portion. The bullet had passed through the helmet just high enough to graze the top of his head without inflicting injury to his noggin. However, the little plug that the bullet punched out as it entered the steel helmet deflected off the helmet liner. The plug raced around inside, and over the top, and down the backside of the helmet, entering the back of his neck, and inflicting a small flesh wound that got him off the front lines for a while.

A short time later we were off the front for rest. We were standing in line for chow when I noticed a soldier carrying his helmet in his arm. I asked him why he was carrying his helmet and he turned it around and showed it to me. It had a bullet hole through it just like the one I saw a few days before. He also received a wound in the back of his neck and had just gotten back from the hospital.

I asked him again why was he carrying his helmet in the chow line. He said, "man, I have had a world of trouble just trying to keep this helmet. Every time I make a turn, or go somewhere else, they all want to give me a replacement helmet but I don't want another helmet. This one suites me just fine. This helmet became a special part of my life when that bullet passed through it, grazing the top of my head, I will not part with it under any condition." That soldier had a very close call with death and had experienced a once in a lifetime event, so why not let him take the helmet home with him if he survived the war. I have to agree with the poor GI. That's my opinion. What's yours?

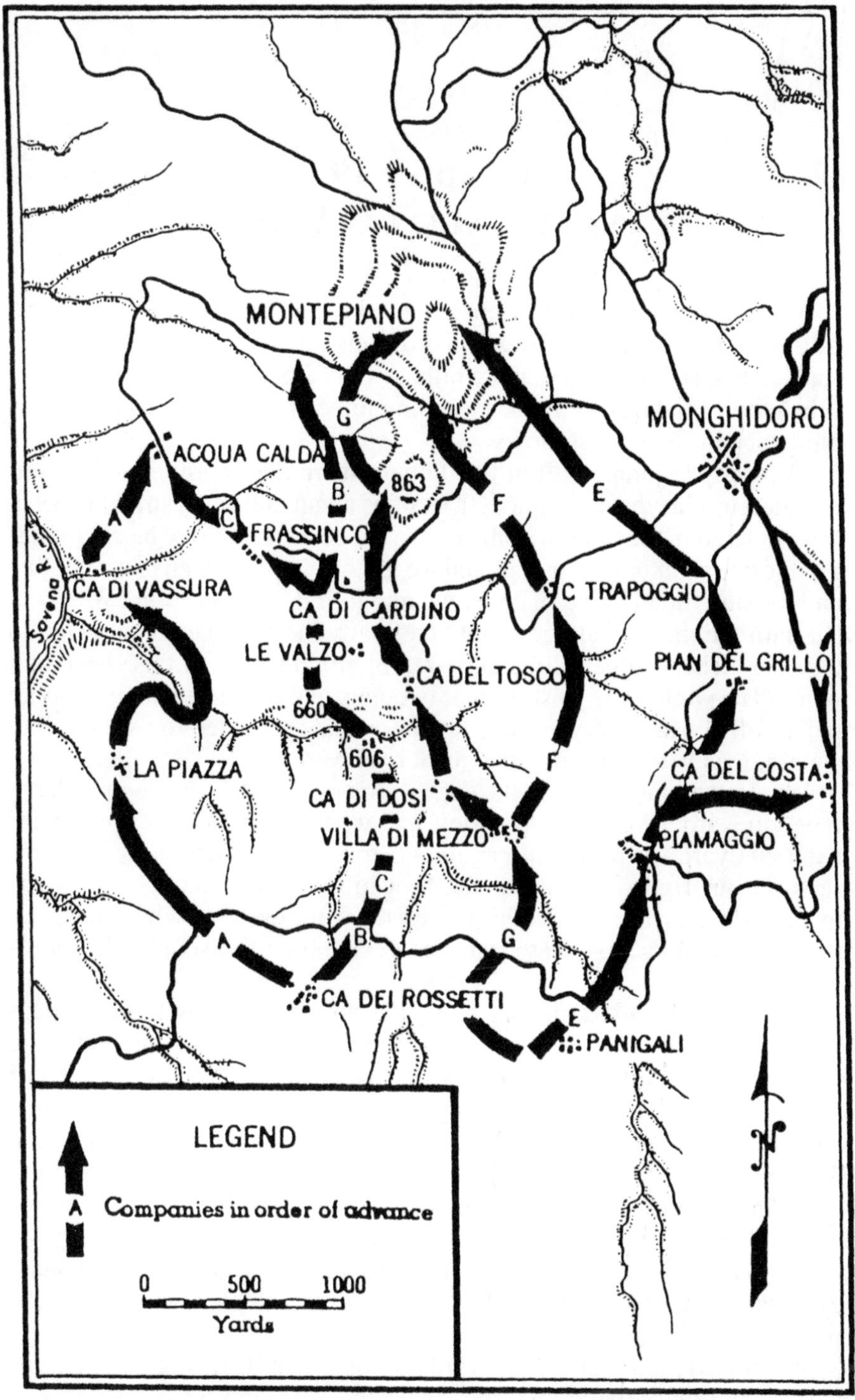

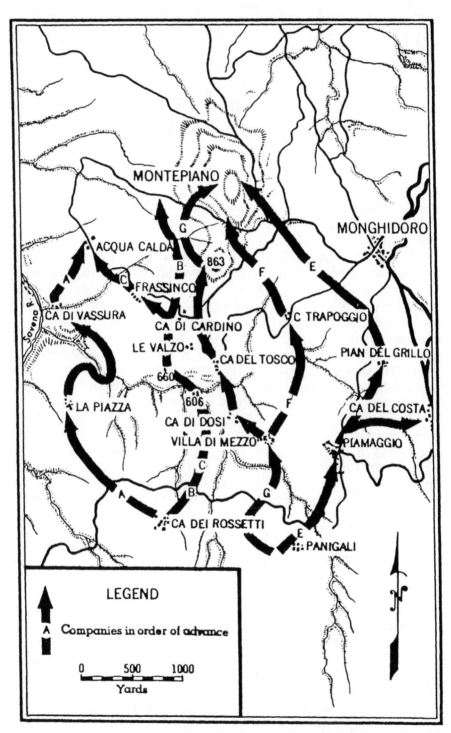

MONTEPIANO
MONGHIDORO
ACQUA CALDA
G
863
B
C
FRASSINCO
F
E
CA DI VASSURA
Savena R.
CA DI CARDINO
C TRAPOGGIO
LE VALZO
CA DEL TOSCO
PIAN DEL GRILLO
660
606
LA PIAZZA
F
CA DEL COSTA
CA DI DOSI
VILLA DI MEZZO
PIAMAGGIO
C
B
G
A
CA DEI ROSSETTI
E
PANIGALI
LEGEND
A
Companies in order of advance
0
500
1000
Yards
N

The Battle for Montepiano.

Chapter 19
TANK ATTACK ON LOIANO

There was a hush-hush offensive to take the town of Loiano with no artillery support anticipated to soften up the enemy October 3, 1944. WOW! A tank attack at 1000 hours on the little town of Loiano. When I first heard of the report I thought that this was going to be great. Yes, the enemy was going to be in for a big surprise.

Company G jumped off at 0800 hours sharp that morning and moved into a deep ravine that lay right in front of us about 200 yards straight ahead. As we entered in the bottom of the ravine we began to receive heavy mortar fire. It came right in on top of us and we hit the dirt and began to scatter like quail looking for any kind of cover we might find for protection. We lay in wait until the mortar barrage lifted and finally the all clear signal given to move out. Then we began the hard trek of climbing out of this sheer wall ravine. The walls were so steep that two men had to help each other climb up the walls. After everyone was up on top and accounted for, we fell into single file ready to move out in combat readiness.

We started moving along the edge of the ravine and came upon a large grape vineyard. We then turned left and went along the outer perimeter of the vineyard for protection against German sniper fire that was coming from our right flank up in the foot hills, approximately 300 yards out. This sniper fire was coming directly from the area where the tank attack on Loiano supposed to start and get the big offensive battle underway.

Company G started moving along the vineyard in single file. About midway through, we came upon a small drainage ditch that ran crosswise through the vineyard. This wide open gap gave the sniper full open view of us as we passed through the opening. The next to the last GI in our squad was coming through the opening was hit in the ankle by the sniper fire. The GI received that million dollar wound. The Medics came forward field dressed his wound and we moved on out leaving the wounded GI behind to be picked up later by a litter team. It is be noted that this bullet injury to this GI occurred on his first day of combat and because of the nature of his wound, he earned a ticket home. That is what a combat infantry soldier would call a miracle.

We moved on out of the vineyard into the foothills facing the little village west of Loiano, between Roncastaldo and Monzuno. Second squad was in lead, spearheading the attack up a cow trail right into the back door of a house that stood on the outskirts of the village. Sgt. McDermott stepped forward and motioned us to move out in single file.

Our squad continued to move forward up the cow trail toward our objective, finally reaching the house. Sgt. McDermott looked in the side window and saw a German in the room. He jumped into the other room when Sgt. McDermott tried to get him to surrender. Sgt. McDermott tossed in a live grenade that rolled under the bed and started a fire, smoking out the Germans to be captured.

A German officer came around the corner of the house meeting Sgt. McDermott face to face. He called out for the officer to surrender, but instead the officer tried to step back. The officer was too late. Sgt. McDermott drilled him, putting that little red hole through him. Sgt. McDermott always said, "Do it to them before they do it to you." I think that is good combat policy. Do you think so?

Sgt. McDermott looked over the next house and saw four Germans trying to set up for a counter attack, but Sgt. McDermott was ready for the challenge, he open fire on them, killing all four before they could get set up to fire. He than moved up and captured a machine gun emplacement and two gunners.

Second squad was waging war in and around the house, gathering up prisoners, while the third squad being pinned down in an open field about thirty yards from our front door. They were in deep trouble with two men already killed and one of their men, Sgt. Jones, wounded. Most of these GIs were new replacements and we couldn't keep them from moving around. I kept hollering at them to lie still because every time they moved a sniper would open fire on them. In other words, they were drawing machine gun fire down on themselves.

To make the situation even worse, it was around noontime and the hot sun was beaming right down upon them. The hot sun heating up them old pot helmets that lay against the back of their necks, causing sweat to roll down into their neck crevices. Buddy when that happens, your neck starts burning like the devil and brother that is when you feel like you need to do something differently. It is a very sad, sad, situation you are facing. You're out there in the open field, pinned down by enemy machine gun and rifle fire and no place to go. Your blood is just above the boiling point, you are hot and sweaty, but you had better just lie there until hell freezes over. It's either that or take the chance of being killed. It is your choice to make and sometime we make the wrong choice.

The days before all of this happen I met and became friends with a big Indian boy from Oklahoma. I had coached him to stay down, and keep his cool, but in the heat of the battle he got frantic and decided to make a run for it. He was too late, the machine gunner had him in his sights. The machine gunner cut him down before the poor GI could reach the safety of the house. This poor GI just could not keep his cool, he jumped up and ran for it, and it cost him his life. The other GIs toughed it out. They stayed put and did not move around. Later that evening the sniper was picked off, the rest of the squad got out safely.

The thirteen replacements our platoon received the day before, now only six left that were combat ready - three of them killed and four wounded.

Sgt. Jones being pinned down out there in the open field with the other GIs is lying out in the open, shot through the butt. This was his second butt wound of the war. He received his first butt wound crawling over the rail-road tracks in Pisa.

Sgt. Jones began to hurt with pain and needed medical attention, so Sgt. McDermott asked me to get another GI and take the Sergeant back to the aid station. This was one big task in itself. Because we had to take the Sergeant down a real narrow cow trail that led down to the bottom of the deep ravine that we had difficulty crossing earlier that morning. To make matters worse for him, he had to lie flat on his stomach, all stretched out on a regular GI litter. After two long hours of painful agony, his old butt was really getting sore. He had not had any medication for over two hours.

When we entered the narrow cow trail, going down a very steep incline, we began to drag him off the litter and he began to scream bloody murder. There was not too much more we do for him, but let him get off and walk down the cow trail or stay on board. He could kindly let us slip him through the rough ridges, and narrow gaps, as easily as possible. He chose to stay on board while we continued to drag him down and out the other side of the ravine. He managed to stay on the litter somehow while he gritted his teeth and screamed out like he was dying each time we hit a rough spot. However, we did finally make it to the aid station that's located in the house where we jumped off from early that morning.

Company G moving along a heavily damaged road bed, our combat engineers had just finished the repairs on the road when we passed through the pass. The Germans had set demolition charges along this road bed and blew off the whole mountain pass.

As luck would have it, Sgt. Jones' injury occurred on his first day back on the front lines. It looked like he, finally, was going to get a free trip back home.

I returned to the house where the squad was being holed up. They were using it as an emergency aid station. Meanwhile, the 1st and 3rd squad was out mopping up the rest of the village. To my amazement, a GI walked around the corner of the house and his face looked like he was from outer space. He had jumped into a foxhole that morning when a German nearby lobbed a potato masher (concussion grenade) right in on top of him. Bless his heart, he tried to get out of his foxhole before it exploded, but he was too late. The grenade exploded underneath him, knocking him unconscious for over two hours. Eventually, he came to and began to wander around looking for help. Fortunately, he walked into our new command post and aid station where we assisted him. He just happened to be one of the new replacements we had received just the day before.

Obviously, he was still in great pain. His face was all purple (blood shot) where his skin exposed to the blast. His ear lobes, eye lids and lips become swollen completely out of proportion. His facial units that were hanging down reminded me of an old turkey gobbler's wattle and carbuncles when he has them all pumped up full of blood. The GI was still in shock, talking out of his mind. Poor Guy, he just did not know what was going on. We patched him up and gave him a cigarette between those big fat lips and after a few big puffs, he began to come back lively, back into the real world. Later that afternoon we sent him back to the aid station and command post with two German prisoners.

About 1400 hours that afternoon we began to clear the rest of the village and we picked up two more, German prisoners. Sgt. McDermott asked me to escort them back to our command post. I suddenly remembered that I had crossed this same path earlier in the day, before noontime, a sniper had fired on me while I was crossing this same open field with two other prisoners. WOW, that same sniper was still up there. "Damn," I said to myself, "Where are our troops that are supposed to be over there in that sector?" Anyway, I hit the dirt and the prisoners followed suit. We crawled over to a small drainage ditch and went down it until we were out of range of the sniper's fire.

However, about an hour later a GI from the 2nd squad whom I will call Fred, was bringing back two German prisoners when this same sniper took a shot at him. He was hit in the back by this same sniper. The bullet struck him in the left shoulder and went under his shoulder blade, causing considerable damage to his back and shoulder. The impact of the bullet knocked him down, leaving him in serious pain. It is hard to believe this story! The two German prisoners, instead of escaping, did a good deed. They picked him up and carried him all the way down through the deep ravine and over to the other side to the Command post and to the aid station. They evidently were proud to be prisoners and even more proud just to be alive.

Next morning we began to attack the Germans full blast, head on. It was raining that morning when we ran into strong German resistance. Sgt. McDermott was caught out in an open field by a sniper firing from an open window. He quickly fired back and ran for cover. Lt. Flesher moved up near the window, and tossed in a grenade, causing one German to give up while another, a machine gunner ran toward Sgt. McDermott's position and he was shot. Later that day, two Germans, radiomen blundered into our new position, Lt. Flesher shot one, and Sgt. McDermott shot the other. During this battle, Sgt. McDermott was credited with seven Germans killed, and knocking out three machine gun positions.

During the battle, we thought we were assisting the big tank attack that was supposedly underway.

A couple of days later, we found out what had actually happened. We knew something had to be wrong because of all the sniper fire we were receiving from our right flank up toward highway 65. It was coming from the same area where the tank attack was to occur. Yet, there was nothing moving in that sector.

The story of what really happened is what we in company G called the Blue Ribbon Panel Directed Tank Attack on the little mountain village town of Loiano.

Two tanks of the 757th Tank Battalion were in the main attack force. The first tank moved into position and started around a sharp curve in the road heading toward Loiano. No sooner had the tank made the turn in the road when a German antitank crew, sitting high above the town looking down on the road, saw this juicy target coming right at them. They let go one round, and bang, and one American tank was dead in its tracks. That stopped the tank attack, plus all the main Infantry attacking Companies all the way down to Company G.

Evidently our Company didn't receive the word to hold up. Company G was charging the enemy head on, sticking our necks out like a sore thumb, and fighting like mad men, (at least like our one man, army, Sgt. McDermott, was doing). By the end of two days fighting he had killed seven Germans, and captured ten. To his growing credit, he would have bottled up many more if not called back. During the heavy fighting in this small village, Sgt. McDermott earned his first Silver Star. After three days of hard fighting our Company was pulled off the lines and went into reserve.

Chapter 20
R.A. HARPER 361ST INFANTRY STORY

The 361st Inf. Reg. was on the right side of Highway 65 supporting the tank attack on the little village of Loiano. Fifty years later I talked to R.A. Harper, a local resident of Marietta, Oklahoma, who was a BAR man with Co. B of the 361st Inf. Reg. The regiments had outflanked Monghidoro and were moving up the east side of Highway 65 pushing toward Loiano when they halted, temporarily, for reinforcements. He described the tank battle from a different prospective.

R.A. told me his squad in Co. B was dug in near the two tanks that went into battle that morning when both tanks took direct hits. He said, after the fire and smoke cleared out of the lead tank he saw a wounded GI crawl out of the tank turret with both legs missing. He went on to say that his squad got caught up in the heavy shelling that followed the tank attack. The Germans laid in 270mm artillery fire right in on top of them (man that is big stuff). He and one other GI got out of that big firefight only able enough to carry on the fight, or at least able to be combat ready.

I told him he sounded like me. When a big battle was raging and the enemy was shelling our position real hot and heavy, I would hunker in my bunker until the shelling lifted. I liked the comfort and shelter of a deep foxhole. He said, "I certainly did too." After 14 months of combat duty on the front lines as a BAR man and not wounded, he had to like foxholes and certainly didn't mind digging them deep and real often. Regardless how you might feel or tired you might become after battling all day under very strenuous conditions. It's still a must do condition. You have to put out that extra effort to dig in deep to survive. Apparently deep digging and doing it often saved his life many times. It certainly did mine. To survive for 14 months without getting wounded had to be a miracle. That's my opinion. What's yours?

He went on to tell me about another skirmish he had with a whole army of Germans that unexpectedly showed up right in front of their bunker. His buddy was on post duty at the time and fired into the lead group. Fortunately, his bullet went astray and didn't hit any of the troops as they came marching forward. What really saved the day for the Germans was one of them could speak English. He hollered out, "Don't shoot, don't shoot, we are coming in to give up." So that stopped the firing.

The German called out just in time, because R.A. Harper was going for his BAR when he realized that they were coming in to give up. There were

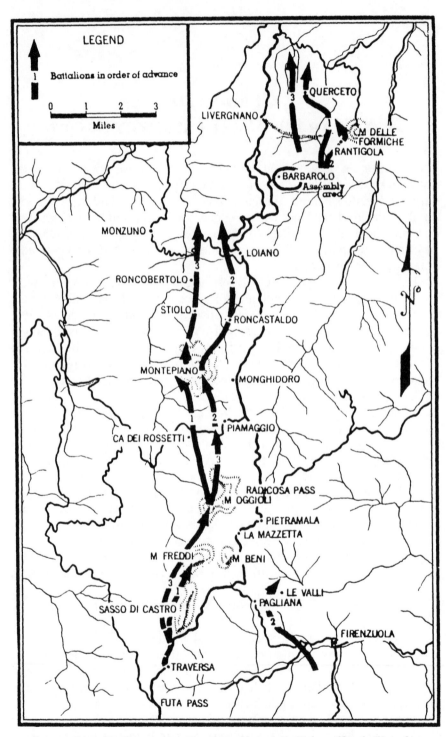

Company G attacking Roncastaldo and outskirts of Loiano. Up Highway 65 to the Winter Line.

hundreds of them. In fact, there were so many they didn't have room to handle them in the immediate area. They become strung out all the way down the hill out into no man's land. R.A. Harper called back to the command post for additional troops to be sent up in a big hurry to help escort all of these prisoners back to the rear area.

WOW! That was a scary event, because they didn't have any idea what to do with so many enemy troops piling in on them so suddenly. Remember these two little GIs were out there in a bunker facing the enemy expecting a big attack rather than the whole German army coming in to give up. R.A. Harper said this was one time he really became scared. These words are coming from a seasoned, combat infantry soldier, so I believe him. Don't you?

Chapter 21

THREE DAYS OF REST AND PLAY
(ADICE VALLEY)

We had three days of rest and play right under the big guns of our own artillery. While they were booming away at the enemy we were having a softball game. That's hard to believe, but anytime we were out of range of mortar and machine gunfire we considered ourselves to be pretty safe. Orders came that afternoon for our playtime to come to a screeching halt, and that's when our blood began to heat up. We knew that we were on our way back to the front lines to start the same old thing over and over again.

There is no rest for the weary, man. Let me tell you something right now. Front line duty is a struggle and a matter of life and death struggle and I struggled every minute to stay alive as long as I had any breath left in me.

We bundled up all of our belongings and moved out on foot, trotting down that lonesome road on our way over to the Adice Valley sector, better known as Death Valley.

We were passing by a large farmhouse previously occupied by an artillery unit. They had moved out leaving ration boxes (10 & 1) lying out in the front yard with loose cans lying around. I broke rank and ran over there to find out what's left available for an old infantry combat soldier. WOW. Guess what I found? A can of coffee opened and only one cup used. Nine cups left, just for me. Are you kidding? This went to the squad. A large slender can of bacon left also, but was open with only two pieces missing, which provided enough bacon for the squad's evening meal. You might think that I am blowing things out of proportion, but let me tell you something, friend. Good things don't just fall out of the sky up on the front lines.

Our company finally reached its destination and dug in for the night. Our objective for the next morning was to take a farmhouse sitting in the middle of a large grove of tall trees. The road leading out the back way lined also with tall trees and heavy brush that provided a concealed escape route for the Germans. We started the attack on the house from the southern direction through heavy brush. When we started moving up toward the house we began to receive heavy machine gunfire from the front door of the house. Sgt. McDermott hit the dirt and started working his way up very slowly crawling on his stomach toward the house. Meanwhile, we were keeping him covered while he moved up to a better firing position.

Out of the blue, a German soldier crawled out of his foxhole and started walking up the trail toward the house. Of course, Sgt. McDermott was ready to fire on anything that moved because of the intense machine gunfire that was coming from the house. The German rifleman got caught up in the crossfire between Sgt. McDermott's rifle fire and the German machine gunner's bullets and got cut down. The machine gunner began to spray the whole area with machine gun bullets, but that didn't slow up the attack. In fact, it only stepped up the attack.

We worked our way on up to the barn and Sgt. McDermott advised me to cover him while he crawled over behind the honey pit[12]. This was an embankment where he could get a better firing position on the German machine gunner when he came to the door to fire. Sgt. McDermott moved over behind the pit and I moved to the other end of the barn and began to peep around the corner trying to get the machine gunner's attention. GRRRRR-RZZZZ-Bang! A German 88mm shell came in and hit about 20 feet from my position.

WOW! The concussion knocked me down. One piece of shrapnel hit my k-ration can (ham and eggs) that I had in my bosom, and penetrated the can and lodged against my belly, burning my skin slightly. Another piece went through my combat jacket leaving a big hole, large enough to put my hand through. Another piece hit my pick handle (trenching tool) cutting it off about midway from the end.

This little episode really shook me up, because you couldn't take this German 88mm artillery gun too lightly. It's a mean piece of artillery equipment. In fact, there is no other artillery piece that can match it in velocity and accuracy. It has a muzzle velocity higher than the Garand M1 Rifle that we carried on our shoulders day in and day out. Just as the shell hit and knocked me down, I knew right then that I was getting out of there in a big hurry before another 88mm shell could come in. I didn't know if the barn would come down next or not. In fact, it didn't matter. I was on my way out of there in a big hurry. I took off like a scared rabbit. Because I knew that a few 88mm shells can rip a building to pieces in minutes and I better not be around there if I didn't want to get hurt.

After things started to settle down, I began to mosey back up to the house where Sgt. McDermott had rushed the house and captured the German gunner. The German was mad because his buddy had been killed on his way back to the house. Nevertheless, Sgt. McDermott advised him this was war, and if he didn't shut up he would batter his head in. I believe the prisoner got the message because he did shut up his big mouth like he was told.

We began to assemble our forces again to continue our attack on the Germans when I came forward to show off my battle damage to the squad. Nobody seemed to care. They didn't think it was a big deal, so I shut up my big mouth and got ready to pull out with the rest of the squad. We sent our prisoner back to our command post and headed out the back way, going up the road lined with tall trees and heavy brush. About the time we got midway through the trees we began to receive heavy mortar fire.

Our squad hit the dirt and scattered like quail. We crawled into the bar ditches on both sides of the road where we took protective cover. Meanwhile, we lay there waiting for the mortar barrage to subside. These mortar shells were hitting too close to be comfortable. In fact, they were hitting right on top of the road bed, and here we were in the bar ditches only an arm's length away from total destruction. After the shelling let up, we began to count noses to find out who got hit and who didn't. Sgt. McDermott called out, "Did anybody get hit?" Word went back that our old buddy in arms, Pvt. Hendrickson, our BAR man, survivor of Monticelli Ridge, got hit slightly, but not seriously. He got hurt just enough to go back to the aid station for some of that special attention that all combat infantry men long for.

Chapter 22
ADICE VALLEY
(DEATH VALLEY)

Co. G moved out of regimental reserve and trotted over into this new sector near Cadi Gennar, and C. Pietrafitta, where we moved into a narrow valley and crossed a small stream with running water. Cottonwood and native willow trees were growing along its banks that provided us some protective cover. I noticed a large quantity of smoke pots burning all along the stream bed. It didn't make sense to me why they were burning. They didn't give us any protection whatsoever. The only thing that I could figure out was that the combat engineers had been smoking the Germans' positions prior to our arrival and left the pots to burn out.

We moved on through this area and went up the slope to get in position for the next day's attack. Our squad moved up along a high cliff with walls extending at last 75 feet straight up. We were then advised to dig in for the night and wait for further orders. I walked over to this high cliff and looked over the lower section for possible extra protection from mortar and artillery fire. It was an ideal place to dig a foxhole, but my little ego sensor told me, " No not here." In my mind, I had decided a German mortar and/or artillery shells could very easily come in and hit above my foxhole and cause a rock slide and cover me alive. So I took heed to my little ego sensor's advice and moved over to a new location.

Lo and behold, another GI selected that very spot, and later on that evening a German mortar shell came in and hit Wham-Bang, right on the edge of his foxhole and snuffed out his life. WOW! Was I glad that I made the right choice once again. I felt like the Death Angel had passed over me the second time. Thanks Angel!

We moved on around the hill and dug in for the night, waiting further orders. This was Sunday afternoon, and we were sitting around on the edge of our foxholes enjoying the evening breeze when I heard a loud boom up the draw. I looked up just in time to see this monstrous 270mm German artillery shell coming right at me. Yes, I could see it coming. I only had time to fall backwards into my foxhole when it came right over me and went on down into the valley below and exploded. About five minutes later another one came in and landed right in the middle of the third squad position. Fortunately nobody got hurt. However, I thought this was a bad omen for Sunday afternoon.

Just as things were beginning to settle down for the evening, we began to relax for a change. Then all of a sudden, all hell broke loose down the hill to our right in this large valley. One of our friendly companies was holed up in a large two story stone farmhouse when a German combat patrol hit them with potato mashers and machine pistol fire. The Germans unloaded all of their hardware in the front door and all the GIs ran upstairs and that's when the fireworks began to pop. The Germans were firing up the stairs and the GIs were firing down the stairs. Every time the Germans entered the doorway a double hand full of grenades would tumble down the staircase holding the Germans at bay. This see-saw battle went on for at least 15 minutes before the skirmish broke off.

Sgt. McDermott came over to my foxhole and told me to get myself ready to make a run down the hill. He wanted me to make contact with that unit who got hit, find out if anybody got hurt and ask them if they needed any help from us to stave off another attack. I got myself together and down the rugged hill I went to the farmhouse. When I entered the house I found everybody still upstairs nearly scared to death. They were a bunch of shook up GIs, but they had suffered no casualties and were very happy that the skirmish was over. I reported back to my company that all was well on the company front.

About an hour later, we spotted 15 or 20 Germans pulling out in single file going over a high mountain pass approximately one thousand yards out. We got all excited about this and called in for artillery fire, but we couldn't get the azimuth or the grid coordination on the departing enemy. We let them get away without being punished for that little skirmish our friends had with them in the big stone house down the hill.

The next day was a day of sorrow for eight wounded GIs that got bombed by our own P-47 aircraft. I was sitting on the side of my foxhole watching a big battle that was going on over in the valley to my right where our troops were attacking the Germans in force. Our company was in reserve at the time, so we had a ring side seat of this heated battle. We could tell that our troops were suffering heavy casualties, because we noticed lots of litter teams coming and going from the house as they were bringing in the wounded. Suddenly I noticed artillery shells exploding and releasing orange smoke right around the house that our combat buddies were using as an aid station.

Just a few minutes later I noticed two P-47 aircraft coming overhead and they made a dive on this house unloading all their bombs, Boom-Boom! It was all over for eight wounded GIs killed by our own aircraft. How sad, you know topside calls this type of action, "friendly fire." I just can't get "friendly" out of that type of action. Can you? Nevertheless, this was a very serious tragedy for our troops. It was bad enough being shot up by the enemy and much worse being shot up by your own troops, but now your life was taken away by friendly fire.

The Germans had tricked us. Obviously, they had gotten advance information on this particular airstrike, and marked the target with orange smoke just like we had marked the target on the German side of the line. When our aircraft showed up they hit what they thought was the enemy target. About 30 minutes later we saw two meat wagons (ambulances) come barreling

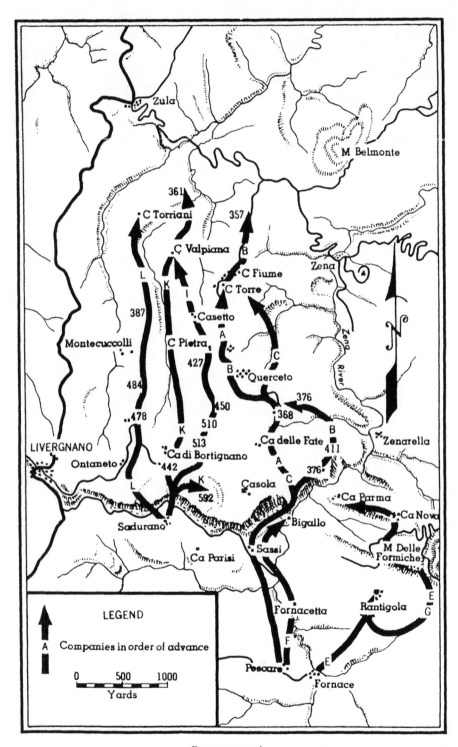

Escarpment tactics.

down the road to this demolished house to pick up some of the other GIs that survived this terrible bombardment.

That very afternoon a group of replacement GIs were marching up this same road on their way to the front lines. One of the GIs stepped out of rank and started walking on the grass when he stepped on anti-personnel mine[13] blowing off his foot. I heard the noise and looked up just in time to see smoke rise up and saw the rest of the troops run over to help him. This was a very tragic moment for the GI. However I must say this about being wounded. If I'm going to get hit or being seriously wounded, brother this is the place where I wanted it to happen! Just like this GI who was wounded-behind our lines, out of range of artillery, mortar, and small arm's fire. What do you think about this?

Chapter 23
FOXHOLE OR SLEEPING BAG

The next day orders came down for Co. G to move out of reserve into the attack position. We moved into the attack position that night. The next morning Sgt. McDermott looked out over enemy territory and saw this large two story stone house over on the next ridge. It butted up against a high cliff making it an ideal place to spend the night.

Sgt. McDermott said to me, "See that big house over there?" I said, "Yes. What about it?" He said, "We will spend the night right there tonight." He went on to say that it made him tired sleeping in these old dirty foxholes

These two letter envelopes with the 91st Infantry Division logo on them were evidently picked up at the Montecatini 5th Army rest center, may be at the Red Cross center.

while the Germans were enjoying the real comforts of life. So you see, we would take the house and have a party.

Sgt. McDermott called in for the normal heavy barrage of artillery and mortar fire to soften up the suspected German positions. Our artillery fire lifted and then our squad started the attack. No sooner than we got started, we began to receive heavy mortar and machine gunfire. Our squad held up momentarily, and called in for more directed counter fire on the enemy position. After our artillery and mortar squads worked these positions over, we continued our assault on the house.

Sgt. McDermott rushed the house and two Germans ran out the back door. They scampered up the real narrow cow trail that led up the high cliff to the top of the mountain. The mountain trail provided them an escape route to get away before Sgt. McDermott could get his sights on them. If he had, you can certainly bet they would have been dead ducks. Our squad moved in and occupied the house for the night.

Sgt. McDermott and I moved upstairs and set up a guard post by the window adjacent to the cow trail that ran right past the window ledge. While sitting there by the window looking out, a German mortar shell came in and hit right outside the window throwing shrapnel all over the place. One big piece came through the window and hit Sgt. McDermott's rifle that was leaning against the wall right next to him. The impact ripped a big hole in his rifle butt. He went over and picked it up and said to me, "Look here what that piece of shrapnel did to my rifle. Why in the world didn't that piece of shrapnel hit my leg instead of my rifle butt? I could have gone home for sure."[14]

Would you believe this? The Germans had built a big log burning fire in the fireplace. The house was good and warm. They probably had set themselves up for a big party, inviting in special guests, but we turned up as the uninvited guests instead and the enemy left in a big hurry. We had a big poker game that night and cracked some wild GI jokes to keep us alert. Our squad certainly enjoyed the big warm house for that one night.

Chapter 24
PRELUDE TO LASSIO/GIGOLLIO

Co. G had just come off of a three day rest period. We bivouacked just behind the mountains in the light artillery sector. We had a nice three days of softball and volleyball games, along with some other stimulating activities.

Orders came down for us to move out, which was always a dreadful moment for me. We moved over to this rich Italian's estate. It had large barns, lots of grain and lots of big white cattle. This was an ideal place to spend a vacation. However, this location was just a staging area for us being reinforced being made ready for the big attack. Co. G would attack this portion of the formidable German defense line that ran from Livergnano all the way down to the Lassio/Gigoilo sector.

Early the next morning, the Paesano, and overseer of the big estate, woke up early that bright and sunny morning, ready to thrash the rich owner's wheat crop. He began by sweeping the large red clay court area very clean. He had his two young teenage daughters come down from their room upstairs and started them bringing the wheat shocks to the clay floor gleaning area. They spread the shocks apart nicely all over the floor. Then the Paesano began to beat the heads of the grain with this long pole-like shalaly with a swing stick attached to give the thrashing pole more threshing power. When he finished that part of the project they slipped on their wooden shoes. That's when they begin to trample the wheat straw vigorously over and over again until the grain become separated from the straw.

The Paesano, then picked up his large wide-prong wooden fork that was especially handmade for this home type operation. He began to separate the straw from the grain with this fork. He separated the straw from the grain and then the real gleaning process begun. He went over and picked up a large handmade basket and began to fill it with the husk and grain mixture. Then he walked over to the edge of the court and picked up on the wind direction. He then lifted the basket up over his head and began to tilt it where the wind would blow through the grain. As the grain fell to the ground the wind blew through it separating the husks from the grain. The strong wind blew the light husks farther out for disposal.

In the final process, the Paesano swept up the grain in small piles; meanwhile, he laid out a large tarpaulin type cloth and ran the grain through the wind screening process one more time. This time it was wind screened onto the tarpaulin where the grain being scooped up in a handmade scoop and put in a large burlap bag twice the size we use back home. That morning's gleaning process generated two large bags of grain.

I saw the older girl come outside, go over to her dad and lean over, putting one arm braced against her leg. She squatted down just enough for her dad and sister to heave that big sack of grain upon her shoulder. She stood hesitantly, for a moment and then she straightened up and started walking toward the stairs leading up to the storage loft. Whoa, what a load for such a small girl! I couldn't believe it. She went straight up the stairs without making one bobble, and soon here she came back down the stairs for another load. "No," I said, "that is too much for her to carry. I will help her. I will carry the sack of grain up the stairs myself."

So I gently got up and went over and told the Paesano that I would carry this load up the stairs for her. He shook his head, OK, OK, with a big smile. I got myself all ready in position and leaned over for the big heave upon my shoulder. Whoa; That was a big surprise for me! I knew right then I had more than I had bargained for. Obviously, there was no way out for me now. I had the load on my back and the challenge of going up those stairs was before me.

The girls began to laugh, because they could tell by the way I was acting that I had more than I could safely handle. Anyway I got under way and made it to the stairs without too much difficulty. I started up the stairs and had to hang on to the hand rail and take one step up at a time. Otherwise. I would have fallen backward. There was no way I could have walked up those stairs without holding and dragging myself along the guard rail. I got half way up the stairs and had to stop and rest. I want you to know that this little offer of gratitude to these Italian people did me in for the day. I found out one thing. These young ladies were strong for their age. They evidently had to work in the field just like men and lift heavy loads to help the family make a living. They were truly honest and lovable people. They believed in making their living by the sweat of their brows. I decided right then that wasn't the way I wanted to make my living, period. I thought this was quite interesting that these people farmed the same way they did centuries ago. Nothing had changed.

Later on that evening our squad was sitting out under a big shade tree enjoying the cool breeze. Chickens and pigeons were feeding all around us picking up the loose grain that had fallen off the gleaning floor. Pfc. Fludd was sitting off to one side from us, just waiting for the time when one of the farmers' chicken's would get close enough for him to grab one for our evening meal. Finally one came right up to him and he couldn't resist the temptation. He gently reached out and caught the chicken and wrung its neck. He became rather surprised at his accomplishment. He became more surprised when the Italian woman of the estate saw him kill the chicken and she came running down the stairs calling out, "Molto stupido, molto stupido." Whoa, was she mad! She couldn't wait until she got to Capt. Conley's office to file her complaint against Pfc. Fludd.

You might have thought that a person was being killed. Anyway, Pfc. Fludd had to go before the judge, Capt. Conley and receive his slap on the wrist. He said Capt. Conley advised him not to do such a thing as that any more. Pfc. Fludd came out of the old man's office smelling like a rose, grinning from ear to ear. He said he didn't expect to get caught red handed with the chicken but he did, and that was the reason he got his butt chewed out.

The very next week, some other GIs in our company shot a big hog belonging to another farmer just a little further on down the road. That story will come up later.

Chapter 25
CLIFFS OF CASALA

Co. G moved into the front lines facing the high cliffs of Casala. Our squad moved into the farmhouse overlooking the valley floor. This house being pretty well protected from artillery and mortar fire, so we bedded down for the night to get some of that much needed sleep and rest. The first platoon moved on down the road approximately 500 yards and occupied a large rock farmhouse leveled by our own artillery fire. The top roof section had collapsed, but left a big portion of the roof leaning against the front lower section of the outer wall. Just enough space left for an entrance into the basement, which we easily turned into a bunker house.

This place was a very hot spot. You didn't have to ask anybody. You could tell by the looks of things. Buildings demolished, big white cows lay dead along the roadway, and large bundles of communication wire ran down the bar ditches. All of these signs are very strong indicators that war is hell, telling the little lonesome GI like me that the fighting along this route had been tough, and of course would continue to be so. This tough fighting will continue until a breakthrough is made somewhere in this formidable German defense line.

One of the most obvious ways to tell that the fighting had been fierce was to move to a foxhole to replace a GI. If he didn't have time to tell you anything about what was going on, then you knew he had been terribly busy. He didn't have a chance to say what to expect from the enemy like sniper, and machine gunfire or any other detail information.

By now brother, you had gotten the message.

If you hadn't, you would just need to hang around for a short while and you would get the message real quickly.

You moved into your new home and started taking an inventory of your belongings and settled down for a nice stay. You looked out of your open window (foxhole) and saw a high cliff out there in front of you approximately 150 feet straight up (sheer walls). At this very moment you didn't know, but you found out shortly, that the whole mountain top was bristling with machine gun and rifle fire. Every time you moved a German sniper would take a pot shot at your head. The Germans had the high ground and we had the low hell holes. You know, that is exactly the way the Germans planned it. The only possible way of getting in and out of your foxhole for a break was late at night. If the moon was shinning brightly, you had better stay put or else you were a dead duck.

The next night our squad moved out of the pleasure house[15] down the highway into the bunker house. On our way down the road we noticed all of these large white cows lying dead with their feet sticking straight up in the air. A young GI city dude asked the sergeant up front of the line, "Hey sergeant, do these cows sleep with their feet straight up in the air?" Another GI in the squad spoke up and said, "No goofy. These cows are only scratching their backs." The whole squad just burst out laughing. The sergeant up front answered right back and said, "Soldier, these cows are truly dead." The soldier answered right back, "Yes I know they are truly dead sergeant, but I just wondered if they sleep that way." "OK," the sergeant said, "lets move out, men. We have no time to spend on dead cows." The sergeant was right. The next three days time we spent in pure hell.

Chapter 26
THE HOG THAT SQUEALED

The day before we left the pleasure house, Sgt. McDermott made mention of a big fat hog that was in a small pen just around the corner in the barnyard. He said, "Man, that big hog will be fine eating. Just wait until we pull our outpost duty and we will butcher that hog and have fresh meat for the whole squad." I thought that was a great idea and suggested we make plans for the supply sergeant to bring up the big fry skillet from the company kitchen. WOW, everything set for the big moment.

The next night we moved from the bunker house onto the hump. Some called it the mound. This mound was a sharp rise out in the middle of nowhere. Actually, it's surrounded by open fields and flat country, which made it very difficult to defend. German machine guns and mortar fire raked across our foxhole's day and night continuously. To make matters worse, the wind was hot and dry, blowing dirt down our sweaty necks and into our eyes, making them burn like fire. It was a sad time for our squad because the only thing we could do was lie there and sweat it out until our time was up. I don't mean death; I meant to say when directed to pull back into a reserve position.

One German machine gunner in particular was always strafing our position. We finally got tired of it and called in for artillery fire be lain on his position. About 15 minutes later we heard our artillery(105mm) open up and were aware that the shells were on their way. Bang, bang, seven rounds on their way, all of them coming in right on target, That's what we thought! No sooner had the artillery fire lifted, when the German machine gunner rose up and let loose with a wild burst of machine gunfire right down into our position. Obviously he wanted to let us know that he was still up there safe and sound.

Just outside of the bunker house, at the corner to my left, lay a dead German soldier. He was there when we arrived and there when we left. He didn't have a rifle with him. Evidently, he was trying to come in and give up, but something went wrong. You might know, up here on the front lines we have happy trigger finger GIs that often pull the trigger. Whatever happened, the German lost his life just a few feet away from our freedom zone. Sorry, he just didn't make it the last 20 feet.

That very night we heard a rifle shot ring out back at the pleasure house and the big hog let out a big squeal and then the squealing was all over. I told my buddy, "Oh, boy, sounds like we will have fresh hog meat tomorrow night when we pull back into reserve." "What do you think happened to the big hog when shot in the head?" The hog did not drop dead in his tracks. Instead he started running and squealing and jumped head over heals into the barnyard cesspool, what the GIs called the honey pit. There the hog sank to the bottom, leaving no possible way for the GIs to fish that big 400 pound slick and slimy hog out of that stinking honey pit. Gosh, I was hungry for fresh hog meat, but not marinated in cow manure and human waste.

Chapter 27
NIGHT PATROLS

During the night we had two patrols out. One 20 man combat patrol was out operating along the river. The other three man patrol was operating approximately 200 yards down the road. They were operating between us and an old mill house located over to our left, along the river's edge. Co. K occupied the old mill house.

Approximately 1100 hours that night a 35 man German combat patrol came across the river and entered into Co. G territory. Standing straight up on the road, they started marching right down the road just like a regular group of GIs. They walked right up to our three man listening patrol before our men realized who these visitors were. Our sergeant raised up and saw these troops, realizing that they were not our troops returning from combat patrol duty, but the enemy. This German combat patrol was armed up to the gills. This little three man patrol was outmanned and outgunned and the sergeant thought the only thing for him to do was to open fire. That turned out to be the wrong thing for him to do. The sergeant got only one shot off when the whole German combat patrol unloaded everything they had right in on top of them. They threw potato mashers (hand grenades) and opened up with machine pistol fire, spraying the whole area as they made a charge on our three man position.

We sent out a recovery team early next morning before daylight to make an assessment of what had happened to our listening patrol. We found them in a shamble; the sergeant killed outright, Pvt. House knocked unconscious, stomped from head to toe and left for dead. The other GI was missing, evidently captured and taken as a prisoner of war. We never found any trace of him afterwards. We recovered the sergeant's body, and managed to revive Pvt. House enough to get him on a stretcher. We hauled him back to the bunker house along with the dead sergeant. The medics went to work on Pvt. House. They bandaged him up nicely, gave him a cup of hot coffee, a big puff on a cigarette then bedded him down in the basement where he could get some sleep and rest. Later in the day we shipped him back to the rear under the cover of darkness.

We placed the dead sergeant just inside the doorway entrance to the bunker house. There was just enough room to lay him out and cover him with a shelter half and still have enough room to post a guard on the door. I will always remember the first night pulling guard duty at the door. I would forget about him being on the floor behind me and every time I stepped back I would step on something soft. I would look back and I would be standing on his hand. This incident would always leave me with a queasy feeling.

The dead sergeant was new to our company, and hadn't gotten too well acquainted; however, I do remember some special features about him. He was rather tall, and had blond hair and a large handlebar mustache. He was probably in his early 30s. He did make a rather unusual comment about his patrol action just before he was ready to leave on his patrol duty. He said, "I've got a gut feeling that these night patrols are going to shorten my career if I am not awful careful." I bid him farewell that night, wished him the best of luck, and told him to be careful. He said, "I'm always careful." Obviously, that wasn't good enough for that very night he lost his life.

A couple of nights later, Co. K remained holed up in the old mill house. A German demolition squad slipped across the river and entered the long wheel shaft tunnel that ran from the river's edge to underneath the mill house. The Germans had placed a large, honey comb demolition charge along the west wall and detonated it. The explosion blew out the whole west wall of the tall mill house building, causing the wall to collapse on a squad of Co. K men that were sleeping along the wall. Every man in the squad killed. It was a terrible loss for Co. K.

Chapter 28
THE CAT IN THE SADDLE

Co. G moved into a holding position near the small village of Poggio. The villages became flattened by our own artillery prior to our arrival. In fact, the company we were replacing had already dug outpost bunkers, so all we had to do was to move in and take over. The first night our squad stayed in the rubble of the village waiting for our outpost assignment. Things went well for the first night with not too much mortar or machine gunfire.

The next night things changed for the worse. The first thing that happened was a German mortar shell came in and hit the backside of the two-man bunker that my buddy and I were going to occupy that very night. The explosion knocked out two timbers that covered the back part of the bunker unloading a ton of loose dirt down on the occupants. By the time we got there they both were still very much shook up. They left out in a big hurry, leaving my buddy and me to weather the storm for the next few days.

We got all settled in for the night, and about dusk the moon began to make its appearance over the horizon, providing just enough light for me to see out into no-man's land. I was looking straight through a saddle shaped ridge that sloped down about 20 feet in front of our foxhole. As I was gazing out, I noticed a house cat coming down the slope. He went right out in front into the middle of the saddle and stopped. SIP-RIPBRRRR, bang! Machine gunfire came right over my bunker. Man! I ducked back into my bunker and told my buddy, "Look up there at that damn house cat. Would you believe, he is drawing that machine gunfire!" The cat moved just a little bit and ZIP-RIPBRRRR the machine gunner opened up on the cat again.

I guess the gunner thought maybe the cat was my head bobbing up and down and that I was playing war games with him. I told my buddy that we had to get that darn cat out of here somehow. I began to throw rocks and clods of dirt at him but he wouldn't budge from that cool location. We put up with that cat until about eleven o'clock when he decided on his own to get up and go home, making the rest of the night rather peaceful and quiet. They replaced us before daylight the next morning and we went back to the command post for the rest of the day off.

The next night we drew the same position, "WOW! It was another night of cat fever. No not quite, but it was a different type of experience, however. At 2200 hours sharp a 35 man combat patrol team came down the trail right in front of my bunker and stopped. This was the last outpost and gateway leading out into no-man's land. The officer in charge stopped and gave me the password and I gave him the counter response that everything was fine. He said they would be out no longer than two hours, and if they captured some prisoners rather quickly they would be back sooner. If they got into a fire fight they would disengage the enemy and head for home, using this same route to re-enter our lines. I said, "OK I'll be expecting you. Just give me the password as you approach my post and come barreling right on through."

The patrol started moving on down the trail and then they came to a sudden halt. Word came back up the line that the moon was still too bright to enter the valley floor. They would hold up another 30 minutes to let the moon get behind some clouds that were hovering over the valley. At 2330 hours the valley became dark enough for the patrol to move out into no-man's land in search of the enemy. The last man to come through was the telephone communications wire man, stringing his wire as he brought up the rear. The patrol moved into the Zena River bed and started the hunt. Right off the bat the patrol ran head on into a German combat patrol and the fire-works started with a big bang.

The whole valley was cracking and popping. At first, just the rifle and machine gunfire, then both sides began to bring up their big guns to cover their withdrawal. Flares went up on both sides that lit up the valley floor. For a few moments everybody hit the dirt and lay still until the flares burned out. Then the GIs began their withdrawal procedure. The skirmish lasted only about 15 minutes, but that was long enough to exhaust you completely when your life is on the line. Our patrol withdrew and headed for home. This night obviously wasn't ripe for the capture of prisoners so here they came full speed ahead. I want you to know these GIs became devastated. As they came through my outpost they didn't have a dry thread on them. They were soaking wet with sweat. Some were crying from exhaustion, others crying because they became bushwhacked, and others were asking for God's help because they just couldn't make it any further without resting. Others were just plain slap-happy that they made it back into our combat zone safely.

WOW, what a night! It was another battle for survival. The last man came through the outpost and the protective gate slammed closed behind him. Next morning before daybreak our replacements relieved us without further incident.

Chapter 29
THE CANDY MAN

We moved into an unknown sector and occupied a village that the Germans had selected to defend. The local people moved out of the village into caves down at the bottom of the hill provided for them prior to our arrival. The farmers in the village had turned out all of their animals to forage for themselves. Chickens and rabbits were running loose everywhere. When we moved in to replace our comrades in arms the village was already pounded into rubble.

The first night I heard a clucking sound behind us over to my left in the rubble. I said, "Oh boy! The chickens have come home to roost. That means we will have fried chicken for supper tomorrow night." Sgt. McDermott got on the horn (telephone) and called our supply sergeant, Anderson. (Sgt. Anderson brought our mail and supplies daily and he also took back any loot that we might have accumulated during the day.) He asked him to bring up a big skillet and some grease tomorrow night because we were getting hungry for fried chicken. WOW! Would you believe the supply sergeant did just that! He satisfied our request!

I remember going out the first night to locate the chickens. When I went out the door I had to step over a 155mm artillery shell that failed to go off on impact. The shell lay there all the time we were there and nobody dared moving the dud. Everytime I went out I had to step over it and I always had a queasy feeling about it exploding. Anyway, I went out into the street looking for chickens. I finally located the chicken roost and made off with two nice young hens. I dressed them that night and fried them. Whoa, were they good! After supper we had our usual poker game and the squad was happy for a change.

The next night when I went out to fetch two more chickens for our evening meal, I noticed we had joined the 34th Inf. Div. They were on the left side of the street and we were on the right side. I thought this was rather unusual, but the divisions have to come together somewhere along the front. So why not here, why can't these divisions come together right here? What was so unusual about this event was that the GIs were speaking German among themselves. Hey, I said. What goes on here? Are you guys real GIs? "The sergeant only laughed and said, Yeah. We're sharpening up on our German language skills because we are going out later tonight on patrol duty. Hopefully, we will capture some prisoners." I responded to the sergeant's comment. "That's all fine and good, but you better be careful because we have GIs with happy trigger fingers and they might take you guys as real Germans and take a wild shot at you." The sergeant only laughed and said, "We will be careful." I left the GIs and went on my way looking for chickens but wound up with two rabbits. These rabbits were really good, even better than chicken!

The next day about noontime we began to notice civilians coming into the village looking over their property damage and picking up a few items here and there. They especially liked the junk food the GIs were tossing out on the street. One of the favorite items was beef bouillon and the hard taste-less candy that the GIs always dumped first. Finally, we had to send these families back to the caves because we were still under German mortar fire.

On the third day around noontime, I looked out the door and saw a filthy young Mongoloid boy about 17 years of age. He was sitting out in the middle of the street eating the GI candy that we had discarded. He had a very large head with only one eye. The boy's body being deformed at birth, left his legs tiny and undeveloped crossed and frozen in place. He couldn't talk and only grunted. He sat upright and traveled by pressing his hands to the ground with his strong arms he lifted himself up and thrust his body forward. He had scooted himself over 500 yards up a very steep and rugged, rocky, mountain trail that led him up to the village. He continued to appear every morning for the next three days for his daily supply of GI candy that lined the street in front of his original home.

The boy's mother finally came and we advised her to keep him at home because of the continuous shelling. She told us that he didn't like to stay in the dark cave, and every time she turned her back he left. She knew where he had gone and since he had found all of that candy in the street up by his real home. There was no way she could keep him penned up in that dark cave. He continued to come as long as we supplied the candy.

Chapter 30
RETURN OF PRIVATE HOUSE

Pvt. House went to the hospital for about two months for convalescence and then returned to our outfit. The very first night he was back we were out on the point in the outpost position together. He began to act strangely and fell totally apart. He first began to vomit, tremble, and foam at the mouth and through his nose. He looked out of the bunker and said he saw Germans out there and they were going to kill him. That's when he grabbed me and started begging me not to let them kill him. I told him to calm down that I didn't see any Germans out there. He said, "Yes, they are, I can see them." Whoa, I knew right then I had a big problem on my hands and I had to do something very quickly!

I grabbed the old field telephone and for a change it worked. I got through to the command post, told them my problem, and that I needed help right now. I told them to please come quickly. They advised me that a litter team would be out in about 15 minutes. "Good," I said. The litter team got organized and here they came. About half way out, the Germans lay in a mortar barrage on them and one member of the team got wounded. They had to turn around and take the wounded GI back to the aid station and then head back to our bunker to pick up Pvt. House. About 30 minutes later they came. Thank God, the litter team made it out to the bunker and this time carried Pvt. House away without farther incident.

The litter team took Pvt. House back to the aid station and never returned to our outfit. This first night out episode, in a two man bunker, sticking out on the point in no-man's land with a berserk GI, turned out to be a nightmare for me. You must remember that this position was in a very hot spot. We were in the furthest position out in no-man's land. Everybody's nerves were on edge. We were a bunch of trigger-happy GIs sitting out there where you shoot and ask questions later. Out on the point of enemy contact, Anything goes, "So be careful," was the password for the night.

What I didn't like about this position was the bunkers. The bunkers covered on top all right, but the door opening faced the enemy. If you came under an enemy attack, the enemy could fire right into your bunker and launch rifle grenades through the front door. The other types bunker we normally used opened at the top that gives you much more protection from direct rifle fire, but you can't see out as well. Who cares if you can't see out as well. Surviving a frontal attack is the name of the game up front. I prefer to take my chances looking up and out rather than straight out. Evidently the open door view, looking straight out toward the enemy was what caused Pvt. House to go berserk. That's my opinion, what's yours?

Chapter 31
FRONT BRISTLES WITH FERVOR

The whole front was bristling with fervor. I distinctly remember this afternoon. We dug in, facing an open field, and on the opposite side were a belt line of trees and hedge rows. We had just run into a German combat patrol and got pinned down by rifle and machine gunfire. We decided to hold up and dig in because the terrain was too difficult to cross while under small arm's fire. So we waited until the rest of the company pulled up in line with us. Meanwhile, we were taking a break when we noticed an Italian farmer coming across the open field in front of us.

He dressed just like the typical farmer that lived in the local mountain community. He wore a dark cap, trousers and jacket, and was about middle age. As he was traveling along the ridge line he appeared to be looking for his cows. It's possible, however, that he was just out for a leisurely stroll or was just walking over to visit some friends. Whatever the case might have been, he was in the wrong place at the wrong time. Unfortunately, he didn't realize that he was walking into enemy territory, much less walking right into a German machine gun field of fire that killed him instantly. This poor Italian farmer fell dead in his tracks and probably lay there for days before his family found him.

All we could do, at most, was to report the position where he fell and how he met death back to our command post and on to headquarters. The headquarters could then pass the information back to the civilian authorities and let them handle the problem through their own Governmental channels. There wasn't anything wrong or unusual about farmers coming out of hiding when the front lines moved up and out of their area. Our company dug fox-holes many times in vineyards, and small farm plot when the local farmer would come out and start his spring pruning and tie up the young grape shoots in his vineyard. Many times he would even start tilling his farm plot by hand or oxen, and do it all without incident. However, one of the tragedies of war is that innocent civilians do get killed.

Chapter 32
THE HAUNTED KNOB HILL

Co. G moved in and replaced our friendly comrades in arms at night in the Idice Valley near M. Ceresa. We started our normal hog-wallowing procedure of occupying those worn slick GI foxholes, getting ready for the real thing. We were in a holding position. The Germans have our foxhole already zeroed in and ready to fire. All they had to do was drop the mortar rounds in the tube and let them go according to their firing order.

This hill was a ghostly site, bald and ugly. You could see and hear every movement made, whether by friend or foe, for miles around. I still remember the first night we had settled in. I heard the German mortar crew crank up their mortar tubes. Plump! Plump! plump! This went on until all seven rounds being released and are on their way right into our position. WOW, what a weary feeling of suspense each mortar shell gives you while you sit there and wait! Yes, it gives you time to count your blessings and makes you wonder if one of those critters will have your name written on it. Wham! Bang! Blew-we! Nope, thank God those seven rounds of mortar that just came in missed me again. Hallelujah, Amen.

About 10 o'clock that night, a night hawk flew up and landed on a small bush right behind my foxhole and began his night chirping. This weary sound made cold chills run down my spine. I thought at first maybe a German sniper might be using this call as a signal to pinpoint my position. However, after a long wait, the night hawk finally pulled out, leaving me to the mercy of the German mortar squad.

I thought the rest of the night was mine. I was all laid back, ready for my late evening nap, when Sgt. McDermott came over to my foxhole and said, "Bonnie Carroll you have been selected to be our messenger boy for the night. Get yourself ready to run across the ravine to our left and make contact with the GIs on the next hill over. Find out who they are and what company they are with." OK, sergeant," I said, and off I went. Just about the time I got down to the bottom of the ravine, two German mortar shells came in and landed right in the middle of the area where I intended to go. I came to a halt very quickly and waited for the mortar barrage to subside before going any further. I finally got my chance and moved on in calling out, "YO-HO, I'm from Co. G 363rd Inf. Our unit is located across the ravine to your right on Hill 603. Don't shoot I'm friendly." As I came closer, the only light I could see was coming from an area near some large boulders. The boulders served as cover for their command post. I walked up closer to the entrance covered with a shelter half and I yelled out this is Co. G, 363rd Inf. Div. Our company's located just across the ravine to your right. Their answer came right back, identifying who they were.

However, things just didn't look right and I began to ask questions. I asked two GIs who were standing against the wall what was wrong, because they both seemed to be shook up. One of the GIs spoke up and said, "Did you hear those two mortars come in about 15 minutes ago? They landed right outside of here, and one landed in the middle of our mortar pit. We had just finished sand-bagging the pit and walked inside to get our firing orders for the night's run, when two mortars came in. One of them destroyed our mortar position." WOW, what a miracle! These GIs were very lucky to be alive, if they stayed five minutes longer in that mortar pit they would be blown into a million pieces. They said they didn't want to go back out there right then because the Germans had them zeroed in. Well, I guess I'll have to agree with their logic, however, the old saying is that lightning doesn't strike twice in the same place. That wasn't my decision to make for these two very scared GIs, who were very lucky to be alive. I just thanked my lucky stars that I made the round-trip over and back to my lovely foxhole without further incident.

Next morning, I was awakened by a wake up call from our heavy weapons machine gunner, located approximately 300 yards down the line. He played reveille on his machine gun early in the morning and taps at night. He was firing right into the German positions without missing a beat. However, I noticed one thing he didn't do. He never used one tracer bullet during all of his machine gun firing talent display. It always amazed me how the Germans used tracer bullets. The Free French, Gurka, and other 8th Army soldiers used tracer bullets very effectively. Not by the GI because we didn't like to over expose our position.

Chapter 33
SUNDAY MORNING UP FRONT

You're sitting in your foxhole up front dodging bullets and you are wondering how in this man's world would you ever know for sure that it was Sunday morning up front. Most absurdly you can tell if you are in a holding position and can stay put long enough for our propaganda machine be moved in and set up. The front lines are normally quite around Easter and Christmas time and that's when they move in the propaganda machines to announce these programs. Usually, the morning starts off with some type of church music and a short prayer lesson for the GIs' benefit. Then the German language propaganda portion comes on with German music followed by our announcer coming on to make his pitch.

"Good morning Comrades," He would say, it's Sunday morning and the front is peaceful and quiet. We know the war is winding down and Germany is being destroyed each day you fight. We don't want you destroyed, so we are making you a real promise, listen very closely, we promise you free passage through our lines. You will have a warm bed to sleep in tonight, hot meals, and medical attention. You can even keep all of your personal belongings as well; just like being at home. All you have to do is just drop your rifle, put your hands over your head and start walking toward our lines and we will meet you with open arms. Sometimes this works and sometimes it backfires. I remember on one occasion the German officer in charge evidently didn't like what he was hearing, and more so, what we were telling his troops. He merely directed artillery fire full blast right over in the area where the propaganda trucks and loud speakers are located. Fortunately the broadcasting station and truck survived the bombardment and after a short pause the broadcasting station cranked up its machine and started broadcasting propaganda once again. Usually there is a death penalty for any German soldier caught with an American pamphlet found on his body that guarantees him free passage through our lines. However, no matter how stiff the penalty, a few German soldiers[16] took the chance and made it through our lines to safety. Others took the chance but were less fortunate they got shot in the back as they tried to escape to freedom.

Chapter 34
GHOST RIDERS IN THE SKY

The third day went well. The machine gunner had played taps and we were ready for bed when I noticed a dark snow cloud moving in over a mountain range just to the north of us. Simultaneously, our aircraft beacon lights came on, their bright light beams streaking across the northern sky, lighting up the front for friends and foes alike. However, the main purpose of the big beacon lights was to guide the way for our truck drivers and mule skinners who were bringing up supplies to the front lines at night. These bright beams were bouncing off of the dark snow clouds as they came rolling in, creating havoc right before my eyes. They looked like ghost riders in the sky.

I knew this was only a phenomenon, but nevertheless, it made me feel like a miracle was about to happen. I wanted to reach right up there and hang on to one of them dudes and ride right out of there. Unfortunately that didn't happen. "No, buddy," said my little ego sensor. "That's only wishful thinking." Man! I even thought about reaching out and extending my rifle butt out across no man's land, like Moses did. Moses stretched out his rod in hand toward the Red Sea and God did the rest. All I had to do here was tell the enemy. "Let's stop killing right now, lay down our arms, go home and have peace for ever more." Although, I was willing to do just that, unfortunately, nothing changed the horrible situation I was in. Again my little ego sensor said, "No buddy, you might as well sit tight until your replacement arrives later on tonight."

We had already been here for three long days and nights. We were facing the enemy with heavy combat action, heavy exchange of artillery and mortar fire. The Germans were continuously raking across our foxhole with withering machine gunfire. I said this to myself, brother it will be a miracle If I get out of this God forsaken place alive. Fortunately with God's help I made out safely.

Later that night I walked approximately two miles to the rear area and loaded on a truck for a ride back to our special retreat area, just outside of artillery range.

Sgt. McDermott came by early the next morning telling us that we were going to have a real treat tomorrow. I said, "Great, what is it going to be?"

He said, "You'll have to wait and find out for yourself." The next morning we fell out for roll call and inspection. The inspection being made and then they told us to load up on trucks at 0800 hours and go down to the portable shower unit for a fresh hot shower. We also received some new winter underclothing, and came back to our area and received the greatest gift of all, mail from home.

Now buddy that's living. How sweet it is! Just being off the front lines for a few days is a real treat itself. There is nothing more miserable than being on the front line's day in and day out when its raining and cold. You're wet, dirty and chilled to the bone, under constant enemy fire and no place to go but forward when time comes to attack.

There is something mysterious about all of this, because you don't know if your life's being spared another day or not. Although ever GI being completely exhausted and our company continues to suffer heavy casualties, however that doesn't seem to matter. What matter's most is to move out and attack the enemy on the next hill, occupy it, and dig in for the night. Next morning you're ready to start the attack all over again. Believe me man, there are no ifs, ands, or buts, about it because you know that somebody's bound to get hurt in the next skirmish we have with the enemy. That time will be the very next time we make a frontal attack on that bare rugged hill position. Hopefully, that person won't be me lying dead up there on that lonely bare hill. Lying there waiting for the grave registrars to come along with a white mattress cover to haul me off to the stiff-parlor.

This very thing happened to my friend and combat buddy John R. Burklow from Sweetwater, Texas assigned to Co. E. John met his death while charging up Monticelli Ridge over in his sector. He got hit and knocked down by machine gunfire and seriously wounded. He hit the dirt and began to cry out for help but he was to far out of reach. He was also under heavy machine gun and rifle fire and no one could get to him to try and save him. He lay out there for an hour or more on that bare hill, begging for God's mercy and help from his combat buddies, but no one came to his rescue. Finally, God called him home. He died a horrible death, and this very type of death always haunted me. I certainly didn't want be caught out there like that. Don't you agree?

There is nothing like it, man. Nothing is more devastating to me than being a combat infantry soldier. Ernie Pyle, the combat infantryman's front line friend and foxhole buddy once said, "All the troops up front want to be in the rear and all the troops in the rear want to be up front." Yes, that statement has meaning all right, but I somewhat disagree with his conclusion.

The GIs in the rear areas have no idea what's going on up front. When a big battle is raging and heavy causalities being inflicted, and it makes the headlines in the *Stars and Stripes* newspaper. Only then will the GI in the rear area take notice, become aware of a big problem, and become anxious to help those on the front line. That sentimental feeling will leave the GI in a big hurry after being under heavy shelling from artillery, mortar fire, withering machine gun and rifle fire. You can bet on it. That's my opinion. What's yours?

Chapter 35
COMPANY COOK 88TH INFANTRY DIVISION

Floyd Flatt was reared south of Leon, Oklahoma in a small country farming community. He grew up to be rather small in stature. He was a red-headed, freckle-faced youngster. He was drafted just like I was but instead of being an Infantry soldier he trained to be a cook in a rifle unit. It was not a bad trade in time of war.

I remember receiving a letter from home advising me that Floyd was in Italy. He was assigned to the 88th Inf. Div. as a cook, and the next time I had some time off to be sure and go by and see him.

Finally our company pulled off the front for a few days and I took time out to go over to his unit to see him. Lo and behold he volunteered to go up front as a litter team bearer to assist in the evacuation of the seriously wounded GIs off of the battlefield. About the time the litter team was ready to evacuate the wounded, the Germans began to shell the hill with heavy mortar fire. Floyd got wounded and was carried off the hill by another litter team. He was taken directly to the hospital for medical treatment, and he was still there when I paid my first visit.

About two months later I was off the front again and decided to go over and see him again. Lo and behold, this guy had volunteered again to go up and help out like he did before. Yes, you guessed right. This time seriously wounded to the extent that he went home to the good old USA for medical treatment.

Now let's look at this GIs military record: He was up front each time on a mercy mission. He wasn't carrying a gun. He was up front only to help remove the wounded from the battlefield during a lull in the battle. However, both times hit with shrapnel and removed from the battlefield by one of his own litter teams. This GI being wounded told me something: "If you don't want to get hurt or killed, you had better stay off of the front lines. There was no way you could have stayed alive walking around up front when the Germans had their big eyes and gun sights zeroed in on this hill. When a big battle had been raging, and the Germans knew that there were still a lot of good juicy targets left to shoot at, they would wait just for the right moment. It was usually when our litter teams came in and started walking around over-exposing themselves to the German mortar squad while picking up the wounded to be evacuated. Meanwhile, the Germans were ready to let loose a big salvo of mortar fire right in on top of these mercy teams. There was still too much shelling going on from both sides to be safe. So somebody had to bite the bullet and do the dirty work in times like these, so why not Pfc. Floyd Flatt?

Bless his cotton-picking heart. He did survive the shelling both times, but he suffered greatly for his good deeds. He was a cook, not a sharpshooter. Otherwise, he would have been back in the rear area cooking up hot chow for the troops, and/or been in a foxhole like other riflemen that survived the initial battle. Floyd spent the latter part of his life in a mental institution suffering from deep depression problems. For his action in combat he received two purple hearts and the bronze star for his bravery. Not bad for a cook!

Chapter 36
IRWIN MOTNER STORY

Irwin Motner was born and reared in Vienna, Austria until he was 12 years old. His father and mother were Jewish. His father traveled all over Europe buying and selling fine jewelry to the wealthy before Hitler took over Austria. Irwin said his father got drafted into the Austrian army during the first World War. He fought on the Austrian front against the Italians where he got seriously wounded and lost his right leg. Irwin was hopeful and thought maybe the Nazi's might spare his dad's life since he was a war veteran. Unfortunately that didn't happen.

When Hitler took over Austria, Irwin's dad realized at that very moment it was time for him to make a move in order to save his family. Irwin said his father made contact with the underground French Marquis in Switzerland to get them out of Germany. His father paid the Marquis his fortune to smuggle his mother, sister and himself out of the country. The Marquis smuggled them through Switzerland, France, and over to the Cherbourg Peninsula where they crossed the English Channel to England. When they arrived at the channel for evacuation they were being met by two Frenchmen in a very small fishing boat. Irwin said his mother began to cry when she saw this small fishing boat, because she thought it would be more dangerous crossing the channel in this little boat than the German Nazi's themselves.

The French Marquis only laughed and said, the smaller the boat the better the chances of escaping the country. The French Gendarme thinks we are out fishing at night to catch those special fish that feed only at night. The skipper of the boat threw a life vest out to them and that seemed to have settled his mothers' nerves somewhat. He went on to say, after they had seated themselves down in the front of the little boat and being covered quickly with a tarpaulin and away they went across the channel to freedom. Irwin said it was a long night, and a very dreary trip crossing the channel. However, under the circumstances, it was worth every bit of it and then some.

They arrived in England and started the long immigration process. His mother agreed to let his sister go and live with an aunt that lived in Palestine. He and his mother would travel to the good old USA and seek citizenship. They moved to Toledo, Ohio and established residence there. Irwin entered junior high school at age 12 and went on to finish high school and soon thereafter entered college. During his first year of college Uncle Sam came calling. He was called in and processed and sent off and trained like all the rest of our young soldiers.

Irwin Motner was the first combat soldier I met in combat on the front lines, and we became close combat buddies from that time on. I will never forget the Sunday morning he was busy in a poker game and asked me to run out and pick up a some propaganda leaflets that our artillery shells had just released over enemy territory. Some of the leaflets got caught up in the wrong wind direction and drifted back into our own territory.

Now will the real Irwin Motner stand up and step forward: The GI that wanted to look at the pictures on the propaganda leaflets that floated back into our lines. The GI wounded on Monticelli Ridge and was assisted off by a fellow youngster that grew up in Vienna, Austria, near Irwin Motner's home. He was a German soldier, and now Irwin was an American soldier. This encounter was quite confusing to the German youngster because Motner spoke the same brogue and accent that he did. Irwin wore three different hats: He was an Austrian Jew who spoke Hebrew, an Austrian German who spoke German, and an Austrian American who spoke English.

Irwin was rather timid and shy in his behavior. He always stood back and let the other GIs move ahead of him in the chow line. I considered him more of a loner than the average GI. What I noticed most unusual about him was the way he wore his pants' legs in his boots. He wore them straight legged just like the old German officers wore their boot pants.

I remember around Christmas time we were in Monicatina for seven days rest and we went shopping for a gift for my spouse. I was looking at mosaic rings and dress pins. He asked me to help him pick out something for his mother. I told him what about some jewelry, and he said, "I know, she has all kinds of fine jewelry, and I know she wouldn't like that cheap stuff." OK then, what about a nice silk handkerchief? He said, "OK, that sounds like a winner." So we selected the silk handkerchief for his mother, and I selected the mosaic ring and breast pin for my spouse. After we purchased our gifts we went on our merry happy way.

We went out strolling one afternoon through the area and came upon this large tent that had a large burning candle on a big table inside. I noticed Irwin peeking inside, and I asked him, "Should we go inside and look around?" He said to me, everything that's going on inside the tent is being spoken in Hebrew and I wouldn't understand anything that's being said. I said, no kidding, how did you know that? He said he had seen tents like that before. I said to myself, "He must be Jewish."

I remember on another occasion when we were off the front lines in bivouac. Each squad being set up in 12 man tents getting all bedded down for the Christmas holidays. Great things were beginning to happen; we had just received our mail and Christmas packages. Of course, you know how all of these goodies pile up while you're out fighting the war.

The next day was our "Christmas Day Dinner," with turkey and dressing and all the trimmings. "WOW," what a great day this will be. "Yes sir," we are all ready for this big dinner. Bring it on, man; bring it on. We are plenty hungry, just pile it on, brother. Unfortunately, that very evening was when the terrible news broke. The Germans attacked in force in Belgium and Christmas Dinner was served early. We began to break camp and gather up all our belongings and get ready to board trucks the next evening and head north to the front lines.

We began to move our hay bedding out the next morning when I noticed these letters laying underneath the hay that was covered with our shelter halves we shared during our short stay at the Villanova Castle Estate. These letters were written in a language that I didn't understand. So I began to ask different GIs about these letters, and finally here come my friend Irwin Motner, who said that those letters belonged to him. I said to him, Irwin since you are the guy that caused all of the confusion around here take these letters and put them away. Do this before you have to answer hundreds of question about the funny hand writing in your letters.

I asked him later about those letters and that's when he told me about his real life. The letters were from his sister living in Palestine, and written in Hebrew. He went on to say that I was the only person he ever talked to about his exciting life. I thought this was quite an honor for him to reveal his life story to me. I became completely flabbergasted because he had so much confidence and trust in me.

The next day we had our dinner early and boarded trucks and headed north on that rigorous truck ride back to the front lines. As we were going north we began to run into the First Armored Tank units coming south to the port city of Leghorn. They headed for Southern France and on to the battle-field in Belgium, to stop gap (fill the losses our armored units suffered when they met the German offensive head on). About two weeks later our unit pulled off the front and we really enjoyed the Christmas spirit.

Chapter 37
PAY DAY UP FRONT (ADICE VALLEY)

Our 1st sergeant and acting paymaster, Charles W. Holan, alerted the GIs in our company to start forming a line to receive their pay. Paydays were without fanfare up front because we had no place to go for our shopping pleasures. WOW, they were great anyway. We had a big tent to walk in to and approach the paymaster, give him the big salute and collect our miserable front line pay. It wasn't totally miserable because we did make more money than the noncombatants. Infantry soldiers receive 10 percent combat pay and no place to spend it. Now partner, that's what I call special treatment.

The big payday up front was a prelude to the big poker games that follow. That was about all there was to do with the money. However, this payday turned out to be more tragic than usual. Our 1st sergeant came out of the house where our company commander had set up his command post. He walked over to the tent to inspect the pay table and make sure everything was in place for the paymaster. No sooner had the sergeant entered the tent when, wham-bang, two German 88s came in and one hit about 20 feet from the tent. One small piece of shrapnel penetrated the tent where the sergeant was standing. It hit him in the back but he didn't show much pain as he walked out of the tent over to the house.

He had stepped up to the front door while the paymaster met him about halfway across the room. The paymaster asked him if he was hurt. The sergeant only smiled and said, "No, I don't believe I'm hurt very badly. I only got a small piece of shrapnel in my back and it feels like it is under my left shoulder blade." He took one more step forward and slumped to the floor, dead in front of the paymasters' feet. It was a terrible shock to all of us because we didn't see him very often, and when we did, he was always very friendly. He was a very likable person who rendered good service to us all. He's gone, but not forgotten.

Chapter 38
REPLACING THE GURKA TROOPS

Before we moved up front to replace the Gurka troops, one officer and two noncommissioned officers went forward to get acquainted. The officer and the noncoms made the trip up front and came back with the following instructions:

(1) Do not sell or trade poison can heat to the Gurka troops under any condition. "Why can't we trade with them?" we asked. They explained that the Gurka troops eat this poison can heat and get high as a kite. They said that they loved it and they might even try to trade their bolo knife for a big can. Under no circumstance were we to sell or trade canned heat to them.

(2) All GIs will sleep with their combat boots and GI helmet on at all times. Again we asked, "Why?" The officer in charge began to explain. He said that Gurka troops are famous for their ability to infiltrate behind the enemy lines at night and do their dirty work by cutting the enemies' throats. The Gurka could distinguish between enemy and friendly foe just by the feel of a GI helmet, and combat boots. So it was in the best interest to keep them on at all times.

The next day we got orders to board trucks and head north to the British sector where we would replace the Gurka troops, who had just made a frontal assault on the Germans. The Germans counterattacked the Gurka and, in doing so the Gurka ran out of ammunition and had to use their bolo knifes to survive. However, bolo knives, against bullets, do not win battles. The Gurkas were nearly wiped out.

In this sector, our company was facing a large hill containing heavy underbrush. There was no way of knowing what the enemy strength was on the hill. As we moved into position to attack, our officer advised us to fix bayonets. Gosh, this was a big change in our attack procedure because we had never before had such an order. This order rather shook me up because of this major change in our attack plan. Fixed bayonet. Why fixed bayonets? Are we going for the bayonet charge only to get wiped out like the Gurka's did? We surely hoped not.

As we began to move in closer, we moved through a Canadian tank unit. Suddenly we came to a halt and were advised to hold up and wait for further instructions. I looked up and noticed a group of young Canadian soldiers sitting on top of their tank turret, watching us move through into position. One of the soldiers began to talk to me about combat duty and how he felt about having to fight with the British 8th Army[17] and not able to fight with the American Army. He said he only lived about 20 miles inside the Canadian border and came across with his parents many times to shop. He felt as American as we did. He went on to say that they had most all of our American equipment (tanks, trucks, jeeps, etc. "You name it, we have it," he said. "We even smoke your cigarettes. In fact, we are as American as apple pie. But you know how it is under British 8th army rules. You do as the British do, and we don't like that one bit. "Yeah," I said. "I'll have to agree with you right now because that's the way it is. It's up to you guys to make that change, not me." However, after 50 odd years have past, I agree with him more now than ever before.

Orders came down for us to make the dreadful frontal assault on that heavy fortified position. The officer in charge passed word back for us to expect the worst. The attack started just before sundown, giving us just enough time to take the hill and dig in for the night. As we moved up the hill we started to receive only light enemy small arms fire, which turned out to be a great relief for our squad. The Germans had decided to pull-off without a big fire fight. Brother, that's the way I liked to take strong enemy fortified positions, plain and simple, without a fire fight. We all lived longer under conditions like that. That's what combat's all about, defeat the enemy and stay alive.

We moved on up the hill, dug in for the night and waited for our supplies and support elements to catch up with us. Meanwhile, we had to continue to sleep with our combat boots and helmet on at all times, and make doubly sure that we kept our canned heat out of sight because we knew the Gurka troops would take our canned heat for sure.

For the next two nights the Free French had dug in next to us, just across a small ravine over to our right. These troops were very noisy. They beat and banged pots and pans all night long, built fires, and made tea just like the British. They also used tracer bullets that streaked across the dark skyline into enemy territory all night long. I believe this noisy harassing machine gunfire bothered me more than the Germans. At least the enemy was farther away from us than the Free French were. I certainly didn't like this kind of night life. Our machine gunners hardly ever used tracer bullets at night, because tracers marked our location and set up our position for accurate German counterfire.

Chapter 39
BAKERMAN - FRESH BREAD

Co. G moved into a small village near the town of Rangtigolo and found it vacated by the Germans. They had decided not to defend this small village so they pulled out and let the civilian population take over the civic activities of the town. As we entered the small village I noticed that the "Bakerman," had already put out his shingle for business. He had his big bread baking oven already fired up for the days baking run. Evidently he had put his word out early because he had a lady customer on the way when we entered the village early that morning.

He was using natural wood burning charcoal to fire up his oven to a very high intense heat, and now he was ready for his first customer. I looked down the street and saw this lady (Madam Signora) stepping out into the street headed our way toward the oven. She was bringing with her a large load of dough bread on a bread board about 12 feet long balanced on the top of her head. I would say that she had at least 12 loaves of raw dough bread on that board. Each loaf weighed approximately five pounds per loaf for a total of 60 pounds or more. All of it balanced on top of her head.

However, this wasn't the unusual thing about the bread and board. The way she unloaded the 12 loaves in the oven without making a bobble was what caught my eye. When she got to the oven the baker swung the big cast iron door wide open. She wheeled around the long bread board and lined it up with the open oven and here she comes with the bread board at a slight downward slant and in the board went. She abruptly stopped at the front door of the oven and slid the board right on into the back of the oven. She then threw herself in reverse and gave the board a little jerk and all 12 of these loaves of bread slid gently off the end of the board. All 12 loaves lined up perfectly the full length of that 15 foot oven.

The way these mountain people in northern Italy make bread is amazing. The bread making process starts out by hand. The hearth fired ovens use local made charcoal and fed into the furnace by hand also. A large amount of charcoal was required to get the intense heat high enough to bake these large loaves of bread.

Bread baking goes back many centuries. An interesting fact is the way they make charcoal. Charcoal made from mountain brush, kind of like what we call blackjack shinnery. This shinnery grows in large thickets about head high. When the shinnery grows to the right size to harvest to make charcoal the Paesano takes his hatchet and cuts it down. He ties it in bundles, lets it dry out just long enough to where it will burn evenly. He gets his kiln fired and ready for the brush burn. He packs the brush inside the kiln and turns up the heat. Then soon as the brush burns down and turns into charcoal size particles he cuts off the oxygen letting the fire burn out quickly, turning the wood particles into charcoal rather than ashes.

This is a primitive process of making bread but it works just like a charm. When the bread comes out of the hot oven it is hot with a light brown color. Each loaf has the normal amount of charcoal embedded in the bottom of the loaf with just enough ashes sprinkled around on top to give the right taste. The texture is rather tough and the outer crust is hard, and comes not sliced, unwrapped, strictly naked. When the hot bread comes out of the oven it is delicious, but after it cools down you can taste the burlap tote sack flavor coming through.

We managed to hang around that morning just long enough to bargain for a couple of loaves. These loaves cost us at about three dollars a loaf, and let me tell you something, "Mama mia, this hot bread was absolutely out of this world." Our squad had to move on out, but we did have time to break the loaves apart. The bread was distributed equally among the squad members, and then we headed out down the road chasing after the Germans who were nice enough to let us share in this bread making process.

Chapter 40
LOIANO AND LA FACHBRICA

I do remember when Co. G came off the front lines one evening and passed right through this little devastated village. We were on our way to Loiano[18] Our company had a short three day rest period inside this old stinky, cold church of Santa Margherita.

The little devastated town we are passing through looked like La Fachbrica. The old church sat right along side Highway 65. The front of the church faced the north where the harsh north winter winds blew in the front door and right out the back, leaving a cold damp chilling effect on your body. The cement floor was always cold and damp. They only issued us one wool blanket to put down, and a sleeping bag on the floor to sleep on. Without hay to put down it made it very difficult to stay warm and sleep at night.

The highway truck traffic rumbled all night long making it very difficult to sleep. Unfortunately, it seemed like every time we pulled off the front winter line for a short rest, invariably we would wind up in this same old stinky place. The odor was always the same; it had a very peculiar smell and was always there to greet us for our short stay.

There was another bad thing about this place. There wasn't a farmer's hay stack that we could rob to make a soft bed down for the night. The best thing that ever came out of our short stay at the "Old Church Hotel," was our monthly rations. Man, what a treat. We would get our two bottles of beer, pack of cigarettes, coke and maybe something special, like a deck of poker playing cards for our squad.

Since I was the official card carrier for the squad, I would pick up the cards for us. Another real treat was wax candles. They were scarce as hen's teeth, and Uncle Sam was always stingy with his candles. We just couldn't understand why we could not get more. They were a most useful item and were cherished by GIs in the army. I would select candles over canned heat, two to one any day, anytime. GIs up front used them in so many ways, especially at night when we were inside a rock house, a cave, or down in a wine cellar. In fact, we used them anywhere when protected from German artillery and mortar fire. Then we would light up the candles and have a big poker game. You know we didn't have PXs, snack bars, and USO clubs up front, so we had to spend our time and allied issued money (scrip) somehow, and we certainly did when we had the chance.

All of these goodies were always a treat for the front line trooper, of course Sgt. McDermott didn't smoke, so he traded his cigarettes for beer. He always got my beer and anybody else's that wanted to trade for any part of his ration. He loved his beer. Before the night was over you could always bet that Sgt. McDermott would start singing his made-up combat songs. The more beer he drank the louder he sang. He became rather comical with his singing. He would start his songs out by describing just how he shot that one German when he tried to get away. When he shot that kraut and he squirmed and fell out the window. He sings about a Nazi soldier charging him and he fires a shot that blew him backwards putting that little red hole through him. His singing went on and on until his night was gone. Then he would settle down for the day and get some of that much needed sleep and rest.

What was so important about his singing? I really don't know, but I will give you my opinion. As most GIs went off the front for a few days resting they seemed to concentrate on writing letters, playing card games, and doing other types of activities. However, I must say for the most of us we were trying to forget about the horrors of the front lines. For me, my singing would be, "Home Sweet Home". For Sgt. McDermott, his singing more concerned about staying focused on a platoon sergeant's responsibility of destroying the enemy and how to stay alive. His platoon did just that! I honestly believe that's the reason he survived the war and did so much with his hand on the trigger and eyes on the sights of his M-1 Rifle. He stayed focused full time on combat duty on the front lines and off, and nothing else.

After three days at the rest center we moved out into our winter watch position about five miles west of Loiano.

Chapter 41
THE WINTER WATCH

We moved into Farne, a small village west of Loiano about five miles out. We occupied a part of a family's home while they occupied the other portion of the house. Our squad occupied the cow stalls and made our bed in the long hay troughs. While we slept in the troughs the cows ate the loose hay that we were lying on. We learned to share our space with the cows. The owner of the home occupied the kitchen, bedrooms, and a small room off of the cow barn where they could receive the heat from the cows. They let us have the portion of the house where the strong ammonia smell came off of the cows hot urine in the early morning hours. Brother, it seemed like all the cows used the bathroom about the same time every morning. The ammonia smell would nearly take your breath away. The cow's dung was a much sweeter smell. However, we had another choice, sleep with the cows or sleep in the cold foxholes. We chose the cows.

Uncle Sam was good to us during the winter watch. They issued us special clothing to work out in the severe cold. They issued us pullover sweaters, with caps and face mask, woolen gloves, white parkas on some occasions, and two pairs of heavy woolen socks. To dig the bunkers, they issued us long handle heavy picks and shovels to break through the frozen ground. I remember the first night we went out to dig bunkers. We had to go out about 500 yards to the rim of the Adice Valley in a remote area. We started out looking pretty good until we came to the end of the street and we began to bog down, up to our waist in four feet of snow.

WOW, we realized then that we had a big problem wading through this loose snow. We lay down and crawled on it, but we couldn't get very far. So we decided that we would have to step up high on the snow and pack it down as we moved forward. That turned out to be a very tiresome task, because about 10 feet at a time was about all one GI could cover before he fell back and let another take his place. This process went on for about two hours and finally we made it to the dig and started our laborious task of digging through the frozen topsoil. After approximately two more long hours of hard labor, we finally finished our task and headed back to the cow barn.

The family that lived in the house had two children, a boy about 10 and a girl about 12 years old. During these harsh winter months about all they had to do was milk and feed the cows, sit in the shed room and spin wool into thread, and weave and knit it into winter clothing. I noticed the young girl knitting herself a wool sweater, and I thought that it would be nice for her to knit one like that for my spouse. So we talked and she agreed to make me one for $10.00. She went right to work on it and had it ready in five days. She used all the designs she knew how to make in the sweater. We had the sweater in my family for abut 40 years. Finally the day came that it had to go, so we sent it out to the Salvation Army for some needy young lady to wear.

The young boy was an excellent skier. He wanted to show us his skiing skills. One evening he got high up on the hill out back of his home and jumped off the cliff and away he went down the hill at full speed ahead. We enjoyed his display of talent very much and gave him all the praise.

Orders came down that afternoon advising us that we would be moving out in the next day or so. The head of the house wanted to do something special for us. She got busy and made up a big batch of ravioli just for our squad the day before we left, and we certainly had a rejoicing afternoon. We pulled off the winter watch line the next day, boarded trucks and went south on Highway 65 to the large Italian estate of Villanova for the Christmas holidays.

Chapter 42
CHRISTMAS TIME AT VILLANOVA

The 363rd Inf. Reg. pulled off the winter line on 22 December 1944 for the Christmas holidays. We loaded up on trucks and hauled off to Villanova, a large Italian estate located approximately 20 miles north of Florence. This area appeared to be the staging area for at least a battalion of troops. A very large (huge) number of 12-man tents set up in company front fashion.

Our company front set up along a back fence close to the caretaker's home. Each squad had a 12-man tent assigned to it. As soon as our company got its tent assignment, we all grabbed our shelter halves and made a run for a big haystack just a short distance away. In about an hour that haystack had disappeared and the hay gobbled up (confiscated) by the occupants living inside these tents. The caretaker came running out to stop the run on his haystack, but to no avail. A nice GI came out and met with him and advised him that all the hay would be put back in place when we were ready to leave. Ho-Hum. You know how the front line combat soldier does business. We would pull out on a minute's notice and leave the caretaker holding the bag.

The next day was Christmas package day. Everybody was opening packages from home. I had received a big chocolate cake in a tin from home all colored up like Christmas. The cake was cut in slices and ready to eat so I took the first slice and passed it around. When the tin came back, you guessed it. It was empty, all gone. That's the way it was, everybody shared up front. I opened other packages and, just like other GIs their presents and gifts were too large to carry on their body in combat up front.[19] So what did you do with it? It's a sad tale, but here it is. You smeared it on, rubbed it on, poured it on, and even bathed in it if you wanted to because all of our precious gift articles would wind up in the same place. That is when we pulled out we would leave it all piled up right out in the middle of our muddy company street.

The second day in camp we received the rest of our mail. The weather outside was really nasty and we all stayed inside and read our letters from home over and over to get the most out of those beautiful words. There is no place like home sweet home.

The third day in camp we received a big shocker. The whole camp went on high alert and was advised that the Germans had attacked our forces in Belgium. This started the Belgium Bulge campaign, and we could expect possible paratroops being dropped in the vicinity of Florence. The last word was to break camp next morning and be ready to board trucks and move north, pronto.

Christmas dinner was served early the next day. Everything was in a hustle and bustle posture. As we began to break camp, each GI walked out into the middle of the street and dumped all the beautiful Christmas gifts he had received from home. It was a very sad day for all of us because we just couldn't carry all that extra weight. We had to leave behind such things as bottles of shaving lotion, hair tonic, bath oil, skin bracer, body powder, mouthwash, toothpaste, and body soap. We only got a brief look and smell of it, before it went into a big disposal pile.

As the pile grew larger, I noticed a young Italian girl, about 12 years old, who walked up with an aluminum container, about a quart-size, in her hand. She was waiting for the chow line to open up where she could pick up a few scraps of bread from the garbage cans. Meanwhile, she decided to take a look at what was going on in front of her very eyes. She became amazed at what she saw coming out of those tents and going into a big pile right out in the middle of the muddy street. There was at least a cart load of beautiful bottles and containers of toilet articles.

She was surprised when a GI came out of his tent and said to her in Italian, "You can have it all if you have a way to get it home." She became horrified at first and didn't know what to do. She looked down the road toward her home and then looked at the big pile of loot, wondering what to do next. She knew if she left it for only a short period of time someone else might claim it. If she hollered out too loudly the whole community would wake up and converge on the pile and take it away. So finally, she decided that the only thing she could do was to go home and tell her parents.

When she got home she and her parents became so excited about what happened that they went to their neighbors and told them about the girl's find. When things happen suddenly like that, brother, the word spread like wildfire. The community came awake and when they suddenly realized that we were moving out they started a big rush on the camp. Family's came in droves to our company front. They brought with them wagons, push carts, buckets, sacks and bags, anything to hold some of that loot. The girl's parents got there first and we let them pick first. Everyone got an equal share, and that made everybody happy. It made us sad to dispose of all our Christmas gifts from home; but, it made me feel good that these Italian people could enjoy Christmas gifts that they had never seen before.

We had our Christmas dinner early the next day, boarded trucks later on that evening and headed north up Highway 65. As we went north we began to meet heavy tank traffic coming south. The 1st Armd. Div. was pulling off the front, rumbling south to the port city of Leghorn. They're destination was Belgium, to reinforce Gen. Patton's battered 3rd Army that was fighting off German armored units that had the city of Bastion surrounded.

We moved on past these units and went through the mountain village of Loiano, and on north to the barren rock hills just west of Livergnano. Here's where part of our company staged for the next few days. We lived inside in two large wine cellars. We were in reserve, in a stop-gap position, so things turned out to be rather peaceful and quiet inside these cellars. Right outside the wine cellars our company got served a real Christmas dinner. When chow time called, we came out of the cellars and noticed being covered with black sooty smut, especially around our eyes, eyebrows, and mustache. We had been using smudge pots (burning oil with cloth wicks) for light. You can imagine what we might have looked like. We looked terrible, so we decided to try a different approach. We let the cellar doors open, wet our handkerchiefs with water and tied them around our faces, mouths and noses, where we could breathe freely and prevent possible suffocation.

After dinner we went back in and lit up the pots and began our favorite pastime, GI poker. To make the evening and night more pleasant, we asked two special GI story tellers (one joker from Arkansas, and the other from Tennessee) to tell us some big jokes before bedtime. These two guys were just great. They never ran down and they kept us laughing half way through the night. They did a great job making our day more pleasant.

I returned to Italy, back in 1958 and visited the battle area along Highway 65 with my spouse, Delorah and two children, son, Barry, and daughter, Lana. We left Florence, and headed north toward Loiano. I told them that just over the next hill we would be approaching the building that the army had used as a morgue. It was the holding place for dead GIs (stiffs), whose bodies were just waiting to be hauled off, by truck, to the graveyard. I had remembered seeing this place one time when I had left the front lines with my unit on the way to Monticatini 5th Army rest center for a seven day rest period. When we passed by this place I had seen two small trucks backed up to the door unloading stiffs, both dead GIs and Germans alike.

About eight miles south of Loiano, my family and I came upon this building still standing with the sign still in place that read Tedesco.[20] This is the Italian word for German. Our division had used this building as a morgue during the war in 1944-45. GIs called this place a stiff parlor.

It made my day when I began to walk down a dirt road to a graveyard. I suddenly came upon a group of Italian soldiers in training. They bivouacked right across the road from the old graveyard. I approached them and began to explain that I had been with the 91st Inf. Div. and had fought right along this very highway. I told them that, possibly, some of the Germans buried there got killed in this very area of combat. They were very courteous and wanted to know more about my combat experience. Time was running short as it was getting late and we needed to rush on into the big city of Bologna, and get a hotel room for the night. I bid them farewell and headed north toward the town of Loiano.

As I reflected on the German graveyard I had just visited, I couldn't keep from feeling sad about those men that died fighting for Germany. They buried them here unattended, because they were not German nationals. They did not merit the same privilege and honor of being buried alongside regular German soldiers in the German National Cemetery just outside of Florence. Those soldiers could have possibly died in the same battle as their German national comrades. Who knows? Does anyone care? As even though a soldier was wearing the German uniform, he should have a right to a decent burial. That's my opinion. What's yours?

Chapter 43
ATTACK ON MT. DE FORMICHE

Co. G moved across the base of Mt. De Formiche, outflanking the enemy, and headed up the escarpment near Ca Nova. Our squad made it up on top of the mountain and began to chase the enemy down a rocky country road that seemed to have played out just about the place where we entered. In other words, the road ran right off the edge of the cliff, or else it started there. We followed the road for about a mile or so when we came upon a dead German soldier sitting upright, flat on his butt, right in the middle of the road. He was sitting behind a tripod mounted machine gun in a firing position. He had his helmet on and his right hand on the trigger just like he was ready to fire right into us as we approached him.

Fortunately, he was dead, and as we walked by him one of our persons remarked, "That guy looks like he is alive." Another GI said, "No, he looks like he is asleep." Another GI said, "Yeah, but he isn't snoring." I spoke up and said, "Yeah, he is dead all right, but I don't see anybody going over there to lay him down where he could rest in peace. My question was then, and now, "Why was this dead soldier sitting there placed in this set-up position?" The Germans must have had a motive. They either had him booby-trapped or placed him there to act as a decoy. They must have hoped his presence there would have slowed our advance and given them more time to get away. You know people do weird things up front, and this one event certainly had me mystified.

Chapter 44
ATTACK ON HILL 358

Hill 358 sat right out in the middle of what's known as death valley. The Adice River runs in front of the hill, making it a strong defensive position for the Germans. We used the river for our own defense as well.

Co. E called on to make the attack on the hill. The main purpose in mind was to attack the enemy, destroy his immediate attacking capabilities, capture prisoners, and then withdraw. Just in front of the attacking force was a high, sheer cliff that was standing in their way. They had to make a choice to either scale this cliff or strike the enemy head on. They chose to strike him by using the cow trails on both sides of the cliff that led them straight into the enemy's hardened bunkers.

The platoon made the choice to go around and charge the enemy head on by going up the cow trails on both sides of the cliff. Henry Ford Bowen (Hank), my old trainee buddy from Camp Fanning days, said the battle for the hill wasn't too tough at first, due to the nature of the surprise attack. However, as time went by, the battle began to heat up. The Germans became aware of what was going on and began to counter our attackers with hand grenades and machine pistol fire.

Co. E went on about their business by attacking each bunker and capturing Germans as they went. Lt. Benchart returned to his home base (bunker) and needed the radio brought back so that he could contact Capt. Carberry at the outpost. Pvt. Anderson left the bunker and crawled up the fire trench that led up to the top of the hill. He was looking for the platoon runner to return the radio. An enemy machine gun opened fire and severely wounded Pvt. Anderson in the stomach and right arm. He was given first aid but refused being moved out or evacuated. He later crawled to the edge of the slope where he was helped down to the outpost. After scouting out the area, Lt. Benchart and Sgt. Akers were on their way back to the assembly area when they both were hit by German machine gunfire that wounded them both. Sgt. Akers was seriously wounded and later died of his wounds.

The next evening at about 1600 hours, Co. E's raiding party started withdrawing with their 10 prisoners and their arms full of war booty. However, the Germans had moved in with a blocking force at the bottom of the hill blocking our troops escape route with machine gun and rifle fire. All hell broke loose late that afternoon and the big firefight got hot and heavy in a big way. The combat officer in charge of the combat team put out an emergency call for all out help. The call was so frightening that the battalion commander got alerted, and, brother, that put the whole sector on full combat alert!

Co. G was staging right next to Co. E when the alert sounded and we went into full combat readiness status right then. The whole front along this sector had become a potential battleground. Whoa, I knew right then that Co. G would have to attack the German forces at the bottom of the hill if things didn't quiet down over there real soon. Man, oh man, was I relieved when word came down about dusk that the raiding party had gotten out and the emergency action called off.

I told my foxhole buddy that I would bet 10 bucks to a donut hole that

Sign reads: Tedesko, meaning German in Italian. The sign is pointing to the graveyard.

German graveyard.

Hank Bowen was in on the big fire fight that was going on over on Hill 358. "How do you know that?" he asked. I knew because Hank was the type of a guy that you would want to go along on such a raiding party or patrol duty.

Hank wasn't a glory-seeker type GI, but he was a cool cat under small arm's fire, and, brother, that qualified him for combat action. There's another good reason also, and that reason was this. Henry's squad leader, Sgt. Ennis Beeson was from Willis, Oklahoma, and Henry Ford Bowen was from Fletcher, Oklahoma, that made them live close enough together in civilian life to be blood brothers in combat. That's a good enough reason for me, what about you?

Both Co. G and Co. E relieved later on that night and went into reserve. I made a point to go over and see Hank while we were in reserve. I wanted to find out if he was one of those GIs that caused us to get upset about the trouble Co. E had over on Hill 358. Sure enough, Hank was right in the middle of the fight.

I asked Hank what was the high point of the battle. He said the high point was when he was inside that captured German bunker and an enemy soldier was lurking a few yards outside and the soldier tossed small rocks into his bunker. He thought at first that he would rise up and fire the German machine pistol left in the bunker. However, after Hank thought about it for a while he decided that might send the wrong message to his buddies on the other side of the hill. They were working their way around the ridge line. So Hank played it cool, and just sat tight and waited for his buddies to arrive later on that evening. Unfortunately, Hank didn't have any more hand grenades to toss out. I am sure if he had only one more grenade it would have put a stop to the German lurking outside his bunker position.

He went on to say, too, that his buddies rescued him later that afternoon. He was sent out later to scout the backside of the hill to make sure they were not leaving anything useful for the enemy. Whoa, Hank walked right upon a young German soldier not over 17 years of age standing down in a fire trench chopping firewood with a small hatchet. Evidently, he was preparing wood for his evening meal. The young German soldier was really surprised. He wasn't even aware of what was going on. He came out of that fire trench with both hands up hollering, "Comrade, comrade." Hank captured him and took him over to where the other prisoners were being held while they waited evacuation later on that evening.

Later on the next day I had a chance to talk to Hank about a comment I had made about him being a cool cat under small arm's fire. I wanted to know if he had experienced any combat situations where he became really scared or when he actually shook in his boots. He said, Yes; he remembered this one particular time when they were attacking a village, the last strong hold between them and the Po Valley. His squad was attacking up a dirt road that ran along a high rock wall fence that surrounded a large graveyard. As they advanced forward up the road the squad leader looked up and saw a German officer and two men stepped out from behind a rock wall fence at the end of the graveyard. They came walking right down the road toward them waving a white flag. The squad leader brought them to an immediate halt and waited for the Germans to come on down before they did anything.

The German officer wanted to surrender his command of over a hundred men if we would send back with him an officer and enough men to show good faith. "WOW, this was a very exciting moment," Hank said, but as they started to move forward he began to feel real uneasy because of the uncertainties facing them as they came closer to the enemy position. The enemy strength was estimated to be over a hundred men, heavily armed, still in fortified bunkers and foxhole positions with rifles pointed directly at them. Hank said, "Man, I just sunk down in my boots when I saw all of those Germans popping up their heads. I didn't know what was going to happen. I asked myself; could this be a trap that we are walking into, or an ambush?" You never know. Sometimes men don't get verbal instructions correct and open fire causing havoc in the worst way.

However, after the German officer made contact with his men, they began to crawl out of their positions from every direction. They formed into squads, and platoons and came marching down the road. They apprehended them and marched them off as prisoners of war. Hank said after this episode was over he began to feel brave once again.

The attack on Hill 358 cost Co. E, three casualties, Lt. Benckart being wounded, Sgt. Akers killed, Pvt. Cletus Anderson wounded and Hank Bowen won the Bronze Star for his action on Hill 358.

Chapter 45
THE ITALIAN LEGNANO REGIMENT

In the vicinity of M. Ceresa, a special regiment of the Italian Legnano Group relieved our battalion on the nights of the 22 and 23 March 1944. They were a very rambunctious bunch of young men, running around like a bunch of chickens with their heads cut off, looking for foxholes to occupy.

They become very excited about attacking the Germans and they were anxious to get the fighting underway. I cautioned them that the time wasn't right to get the Germans hostile (all stirred-up) because they still had a lot of fight left in them. Furthermore, the Germans just loved to attack newly, inexperienced, troops. I told the Italians that the Germans would eat them alive and they should take note of what I was telling them. I advised them to calm down and be quiet and wait for a better day before attacking. I also told them that if they became too noisy and drew mortar fire that I'd be leaving this place soon. I said, do you understand, he said he understood.

About that time a young Italian trooper who could speak English came over to my foxhole and began to chat with me. He told me that his grandmother lived just about two miles over the ridge toward the city of Bologna. He was very anxious to go over there and see about her. He wondered if she was still alive and well. I told him that if he wanted to see his grandmother in a few weeks, he had better hunker in his bunker instead of running all over the place like a wild hyena.

"Now you listen to me, OK," I said. "Just when the Germans find out that we have left and realize that you guys are new troops, they might try one of their old tricks. The Germans might hit your unit with a strong combat force that could very easily over-run your defensive position and eat you guys alive." He said, "OK, I understand."

Then, he told me about his new uniform that his unit issued to them. Their uniforms came with additional markings that he and his buddies were not familiar with. He wanted to know if I could tell him something about the insignia on his uniform since it came from Uncle Sam's clothing excess stock pile."

"Just sit down and be real quiet," I said. "I will tell you what you want to know in 10 minutes, and then young fellow I'm out of here."

His unit's uniforms were a dark, forest green. They were a very beautiful color and similar to the color of the old Italian uniforms. However, they were much brighter in color and better tailor made. These new uniforms were holdovers from the Civilian Conservation Corps (CCC) depression days back in the 1930s. The patches or insignias were very colorful and they depicted the branch of service the young men in the Civilian Corps had been assigned to. A patch with a green mountain and snow cap was for the Forestry Corps, and a patch with a lake, fish, and wildlife, was for Parks and Wildlife. There were other patches for Roads and Bridges, Soil Conservation, etc.

I went on to tell him that the CCC program was very effective in building up our country's natural resources and enhanced the beauty of our nation.

This national program fed lots of hungry people that would have had to do without otherwise. In doing so it also gave many young men a trade, which lasted them a lifetime. As I continued to talk, I noticed more and more of these young troops began to gather around my foxhole to listen to what I had to say. They wanted to hear more but my time was running out. My buddies were already pulling out and the Germans had become aware of our departure and began to lie in mortar fire nearby.

I said, "Adios," to my new found friends and away I went, trotting out the back way to waiting trucks over in the next range of mountains. We were going into reserve and afterwards be trained to ride armored tanks into the Po Valley.

Irwin Motner had just returned to our unit after being wounded on Monticelli Ridge. He had been away for about three months convalescing. The first day, we were out riding on a tank, running field trials, climbing on and jumping off and hitting the ground just like we were fighting a real battle. Irwin jumped off, hit the ground and fell forward. As he hit the ground he hit his sore knee and busted his old wound wide open again. He rolled over and began to complain about his knee. Finally the medics arrived and

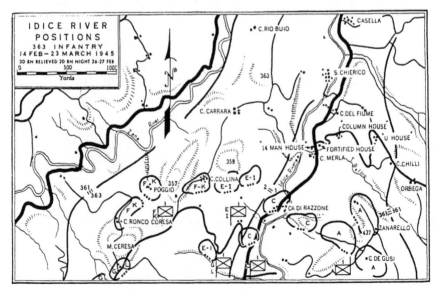

Death Valley

carried him to the aid station bandaged and later transferred to the light mortar squad.

During this period we went over to the firing range to use up old ammunition that we had carried through the winter months. You know. Uncle Sam wants your ammo to be fresh and ready to fire on minutes notice. After we finished the firing range target practice course, we moved over to the silhouette target practice where we used the Tommy Gun. You run some, and walk other times through this course, firing each time a target jumps up in front of you unexpectedly. Just like in real combat. The main difference is that these silhouette don't fire back, so I didn't have to worry about that. I only concentrated on firing at the target.

Capt. Conley told Sgt. McDermott that he had set up a firing competition contest and the GI who made the highest score would get a three day pass to Florence. We were all ready to start firing to win this contest. Early next morning the firing contest started and some of the better marksmen came out with very high marks. Sgt. McDermott was keeping score and was calling out the highest scores made up to that time, keeping the competition very competitive.

Near the end of the firing here came old Bonnie L. Carroll, not very competitive, a poor marksman, and not too enthused about firing. I picked up the Tommy Gun and started through the range banging away at each target as it sprang up in front of me. I was knocking the eyeballs out of every one of these targets. This challenge was like a piece of cake, taking candy from a baby. The other two guys came on through, and Sgt. McDermott tallied up the scores. Guess what? Bonnie L. Carroll won the shooting match. This was quiet remarkable for me to win a firing match like this. However, if this match had been in volleyball or softball, I would have considered myself a competitor with the best of them.

Sgt. McDermott had to go before Capt. Conley and give him the sad news. The winner, Bonnie L. Carroll, had won the three day pass that was promised. Capt. Conley said, "Sgt. I want you to hold everything for now because I'm not ready to make that final decision yet." I had a very strong feeling the way Capt. Conley looked and acted when he got the news that I wasn't a bit pleasing in his eyes. Therefore, I didn't have a dog's chance of getting the three day pass. To the best of my knowledge, Capt. Conley canceled the three days pass part of the competition.

Chapter 46
THE ATTACK ON OSTERIA NUOVA

Co. G, attacked with the 2nd Plt. leading and took Canovetta without a fight. Then Sgt. McDermott's platoon headed for the strongly defended house at Osteria Nuova, where they came under heavy mortar and machine gunfire. That stopped the drive momentarily.

Sgt. McDermott began to move up an embankment when he heard an exchange of machine gunfire and a popping sound real close to him. He said it sounded like grenades going off, so he decided to toss a grenade up and over the small ridge to find out what was going on before he crossed over. It was becoming dark and he couldn't see very well. When he crawled up to look over, he was staring face to face with the German machine gunner. Whoa, what a close call, but Sgt. McDermott was ready for the challenge. He fired one shot, Bang, putting that little red hole through the machine gunner.

Just a short time later, Sgt. McDermott heard the clanking and clacking of shoe heels coming down the trail. It just happened to be pitch dark that night when two Germans showed up at the machine gun pillbox. Sgt. McDermott was waiting for the moment when they ran right upon him. Bang, bang, and two more Germans shot. Meanwhile, Staff Sgt. Hiatt, Staff Sgt. Rosenberry, and Pfc. Rudy charged the pillbox, pumping in rifle fire, and threw in hand grenades killing all four Germans in the pillbox.

The house was heavily defended with heavy machine gun and machine pistol fire. A German, who turned out to be an officer, dug himself in just outside the house next to a large tree. He was the culprit who was tossing out hand grenades, letting them roll down the hill, making all of the noise, and then following up with a long burst of machine pistol fire. The German officer got by with this wild firing as long as it was pitch dark. When daylight came where Sgt. McDermott could see him and level his dead eye sights on his position, he would put a stop to that wild fire fight. Daylight finally came and the German officer rose up to fire his last shot. Brother, that's when Sgt. McDermott took over. At about 60 yards out, Sgt. McDermott fired one shot. Bang! The German officer got drilled right between the eyes.

The 2nd Plt. rushed the house and bottled up 23 prisoners. While they were searching the house for more prisoners, Sgt. McDermott noticed that the German officer was or had been dragged inside the house and two of his

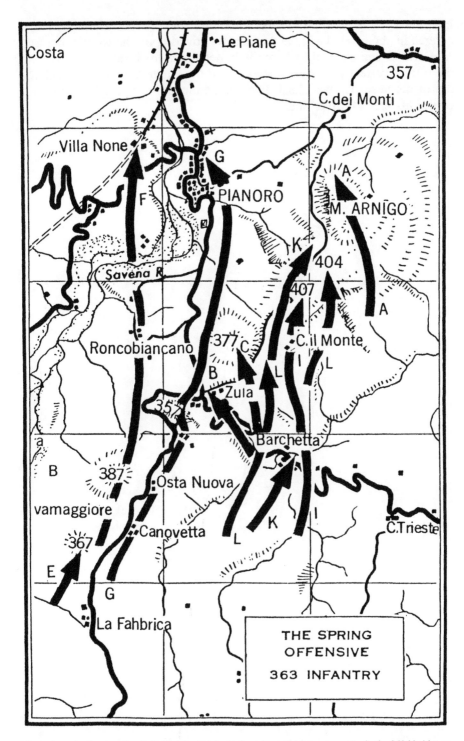

Throughout the five months of cold fighting when the front lines did not move an inch, the 363d held every sector along the territory shown, at different times. During this static warfare between offensives, defenses were strengthened and patrols were active nightly.

men were giving him first aid. They couldn't find the spot where the bullet entered his body. He had heavy eyebrows covering up the wound, but Sgt. McDermott knew exactly where the bullet struck his head. The bullets hit the officer perfectly between the eyes and the bullet came out through the top of his head. He was dead. For this heroic action Sgt. McDermott received his second Silver Star.

Chapter 47
THE GRASSHOPPER SPOTTER AIRPLANE

The little L-5 liaison spotter plane brought up front a real load of value, a halo of quietness. He hovered over our position while he was sputtering around overhead just right on the edge of enemy territory. The pilot was looking down very carefully to seek out that German artillery and mortar positions that pound us daily and camouflaged to the hilt.

Our little lifesaver putt putts along, as a real grasshopper does in full flight. The little plane is carrying nothing more than a pilot with a .45 pistol strapped to his side for his own personal protection just in case he gets shot down over enemy territory. His little plane has no bombs to drop or machine gun to fire. His mission is strictly to hunt and seek out enemy artillery and mortar positions and report his findings back to his artillery unit. He then directs the firing on the enemy position to make sure we get a confirmed hit on the target.

I liked his presence up above the enemy lines that way because the whole front was dead quiet. Nothing moved and nothing went on as long as the pilot in his little grasshopper plane was up there sputtering around doing his dirty work. Thanks grasshopper, you did a great job; we just needed more like you.

Chapter 48
THE MOUNTAIN PACK MULE TRAIN

The pack mules made up the mule train with a total of about 15 mules. These mules were burdened with heavy loads of thermal type 10 gallon food containers filled with GI supplies. These containers were filled with gourmet food such as hot coffee, meat and beans; and, of course, mail pouches full of mail, dry socks[21],etc. All of these goodies were for the front line trooper.

Each mule was harnessed up with what we would normally call a pack saddle strapped over his back. The saddles were designed to handle these special containers. The mules must be young, with slick hair, well tempered, medium size, sure footed with well-shod hoofs. In fact, they had to be the best in the mule population. These beasts of burden had to be able to travel through very rough mountain terrain and narrow slippery mountain trail passages that only mountain goats would normally travel. These mules had never seen such terrain as this before and were trained by special trainers to meet this unusual assignment.

The mule skinners drove the mules and take care of them like they owned them. These selected men were a cross section of nationalities and most of them are volunteers (Italian, and Yugoslavian Partisans, hired by our government to deliver the goods. Brother, these guy's did a great job and our thanks go out to all the mule skinners.

The Yugoslavian Partisans always wore a gray garrison cap with a red star on the front of it. Most of the men were young, in their early 20s, and all wore a real heavy beard growth of at least two years old. This heavy beard growth was the mark of their trade. The mule skinner played a very vital roll in supporting the combat infantry's main supply lines during the northern Apennine Mountain Campaign that ran all the way from the outskirts of Florence to the outskirts of Bologna, Italy. Rugged high cliffs and deep ravines were prevalent all the way. The Germans defended these strategic points like it was holy ground. I mean every inch of it all the way, day and night.

Before the Germans gave up any of this ground by pulling back, you could always bet that they would set a large honeycomb demolition charge on the strategic high point of the road. They would detonate the demolition charge and blow off the whole mountain side, letting all of the dirt and debris slide down into the deep ravine below. The demolition charge blasted out about a 200 foot gap of open space. That space filled in quickly, or a new passage way would be carved out of the sheer solid rock formation in the side of the mountain.

This job called for the combat engineers to come forward with their heavy road building equipment and do the hard task of completing the job. This task was hard and very dangerous, especially so if the Germans got their famous German 88mm artillery sights set on the road building project first. Man, if the Germans got set up first, you can expect the worst, because these guys could certainly fire this weapon with speed and accuracy. These German 88s knocked out our equipment faster than we could replace it. However, our combat engineers usually carved out enough road bed to get our mule trains through without too much delay. Also, the Germans seemed to just love to blast away at our mule train! For what reason, other than to upset the delivery schedule of our evening hot meal is beyond my comprehension.

I sat on the side of my foxhole many times looking behind me into the far distance late in the afternoon. I was watching a long line of pack mules winding their way through the high mountain passes. They're on their way up front to make that special night delivery of hot food to every combat soldier (in holding position) on the winter front lines. Yes, I have seen our hot evening meal wiped out by those mean German 88s. You see, a mule can't get down and crawl like a dog, or hunker down like a camel; so the mule has to do the next best thing. He has to stand still and wait for the best or take off in a dead heat run to get out of the impact zone. It seems to be a tough decision for the mule skinner to make in a sudden dramatic situation like this. Stay put or run for it. That's his choice, what's yours?

When the mule train arrived at the bottom of the hill after dark, they notified us by a runner that the mule train was in. Then a couple of persons were selected to go down and help bring our food and supplies up the hill to the company front. However, sometimes the Germans got wind of the mule train being in our area, and would start shelling the mountain trail leading up to our company front, disrupting our delivery schedule. We certainly didn't like that because we had to wait longer for our evening meal. You know how it is up front, as combat infantry men we became spoiled just a little bit up front also. I remember this one afternoon we received word that the mule train was in and Sgt. McDermott was looking for volunteers to go down and pick up our supplies. This new replacement got up and said, "I will go." So he took off down the mountain trail to the bottom of the hill where the mule train had arrived. He picked up our supplies and was delivering them just outside our doorway when a mortar shell came in and landed within about 20 feet of him.

We heard the explosion all right, but we didn't pay too much attention to it, or about him either. Finally, we began to get uneasy about him, since it was past the normal time to make this type of a delivery. We went out to look for him and "Lo and Behold" we found him just outside our doorway lying in a pool of blood. A single piece of shrapnel cut a vital artery that led to his heart and he died instantly. Poor guy, he paid the great sacrifice only because he volunteered his services for that one time to help out our squad. Let me say this in honor of this young GI. This man's life was snuffed out in the twinkle of an eye right there on the front lines and he hardly knew what hit him. Nobody is immune from death in this type of warfare.

Chapter 49
VIGNA- CERESA SECTOR

We left our bed and breakfast hotel at Loiano that morning. We went into the attack mode all cocked and primed for a big fire fight. We knew something was up, because they issued combat readiness food (K-rations and a couple extra bandoleers of ammunition and in some instances a couple of extra hand grenades.

We moved into our position that night. Bright and early the next morning we started the attack up this bald rock hill, and about the time we got down into a small draw we began to receive mortar and machine gunfire. Our squad hit the dirt. Sgt. McDermott began his usual procedure of evaluating the enemy's firing position. He studied the gunner's manner of firing. Then he ordered us to attack his position without getting all shot up. Meanwhile Sgt. McDermott called in for mortar fire. He had it laid in on the machine gunner while we got ourselves in the right position to make the final assault.

Sgt. McDermott had us wait just a little longer letting the machine gunner raise up to fire one more time where he could get his sights set on him for the last time. "Bang," the gunner's helmet rolled. One shot always did the trick for our sergeant. We captured the hill before sundown and were advised to dig deep and be ready to hole up like prairie dogs for a few days. WOW, what a break! No, it wasn't really a break, more like a breather. We had to continue fighting off counterattacks and take our daily pounding of mortar fire from the enemy. The Germans knew something was in the wind by all the troop movement and communication traffic on our hot lines.

We had to stay in position for three days waiting for our whole echelon to move up. Our battalion had advanced so fast that we outran our artillery support units. Our top brass management personnel tell the little foot soldier like me to stop fighting and hold up. After our unit advanced seven miles we waited for the artillery units to catch up. They brought with them all their baggage, personal belongings, and sleep in maids, and moved up where they can give the dog face GI the real artillery support he needs to fight the real war. The front was real tense; our nerves were always on edge. The second day on this hill we began to receive heavy shelling on our position. Naturally we all dived into our foxholes like prairie dogs. We waited until the barrage lifted and then we were back out on deck taking life easy again.

The field telephone began to Ring-Ring, "Hey buddy what's that I hear?" I said to my buddy dug in next to me, "Is somebody calling us up for a dinner date?" "Hardly," he said. The GI answering the field telephone called out to Sgt. McDermott and said, "Some guy on the phone want's to know what kind of enemy shells just landed and exploded on our position." Sgt. McDermott hesitated for a few moments and than replied right back. "You tell that guy if he wants to know what kind of enemy fire that was for him to get up here and find out for himself. I don't know and don't give a darn."

Suddenly Sgt. McDermott began to think about what he had said, and maybe the importance of this information. He decided to have the GI on the phone to call back and find out who wanted this information. Yes, you guessed it. WOW, it was Capt. Conley, our company commander, who wanted it. Sgt. McDermott just grinned and told the GI on the phone to call back and relay the following message, "I am sorry sir. The enemy fire was mortar fire, sir." That was the end of that little episode. That little incident only shows you how you can talk back to your superior officer when you're under the real gun, and you can really get by with it. Can't you? After a full week in this position we finally received our replacements and went into reserve.

Chapter 50
Tail Gunner On Heavy Bomber

Valton Alton (Buck) Monkres was my high school buddy, who I ran around with during the summer months when school was out. I remember very vividly on this one special morning up front the sun was up bright and shining. The fog had lifted and I could see for miles, even the outskirts of Bologna, from my foxhole position. In fact, I was really enjoying the early morning breeze.

I heard a loud roaring noise overhead and I looked up to see what was going on up there. It was a flight of heavy bombers headed north flying at a very high altitude. I could see the long white contrails of water vapor in the bombers wake. My little ego sensor told me that these bombers were going north to bomb the Brenner Pass,[22] and Buck Monkres was on board one of these bombers. Now, how did I know that! I really didn't, but I had just received a letter from home the past week telling me that Buck was a tail gunner on a heavy bomber stationed in Italy.

My assessment of the bomber formation with Buck on board turned out to be right, but the bombing run or mission was wrong. The very next time I heard from home, my spouse told me that Buck's bomber was shot up over Vienna, Austria. The crew was trying to wing its way to the new air base in Russia. Unfortunately, they lost their third engine over Hungary and had to hit the silk (bail out). Buck said that when he bailed out he could see all the farmers in the whole countryside making a run for him with pitch forks, hoes, and clubs, ready to take him in. That is to say, rob him of his heavy flight jacket, flying boots, and other goodies that might be useful for them to have.

Buck went on to say that these farmers might have killed him if it hadn't been for an army national guard soldier that showed up just in time. However, they did strip him of his winter clothing, leaving him with just enough under clothing to survive the cold winter weather. He said he got awful cold walking barefooted all the way from Hungary to Germany on those cold frosty mornings.

My recollection of Buck was something of a humorist type person. I remember one time in high school we were playing basketball in a county tournament and our team was in the final play off. I mean everybody was really hustling and we called for a time out. Here comes Buck by one of the teammates and asked him if had his "arithmetic for tomorrow." Whoa, what a surprise statement for Buck to make when we had played tough right down to the end of the wire. Do you really believe Buck had his mind on the ball game? I don't think so: the whole team just busted out with laughter. Yes, we got beat by a few points.

When the war was over, Buck came home and enrolled in college at Oklahoma State. After he finished college he was on his way home with a buddy when they decided to stop off at Oklahoma City to celebrate their graduation. They went to a bar and got dog drunk. About two o'clock in the morning he decided to call me and sing me the famous, and popular song, "Jolly Blond." I told him I didn't want to hear that song this time of morning and that I had to work. He said, "No, No, just hold on because he was celebrating his graduation from college and I just had to hear a little bit of that song."

He went on to say that he was drunk, but his buddy was even drunker. I said, "How is that? He said his buddy was down on the floor underneath the phone booth and he had his foot on his back holding him down while he talked. I said, "OK, Buck, if you have gone to all that extent to talk to me, then you go ahead and sing Jolly Blond." He began to sing but he was way off key. That didn't matter. What really mattered was getting him off the phone where I could get a good night sleep. Thanks Buck, you kept me awake half the night, and now after over 50 years you don't remember a thing. Shame on you. I have often wondered what Buck was thinking when he bailed out over Hungary, floating down in his parachute. 'Do you think maybe he was thinking about not having his arithmetic for tomorrow.'

Chapter 51
ANZIO EXPRESS

The 45th Inf. (Thunderbird) Oklahoma Army National Guard Division was in the invasion of Anzio and got bogged down on the beachhead with other invasion forces. They sat there until reinforcements could arrive to make the big breakout sending them up the boot to Rome.

Thurman Monkres, (older brother to Valton Monkres, the tail gunner, later stationed in Italy). He was my older friend and boyhood barber, who cut my hair for five cents. If I didn't have a nickel it was free. Thurman volunteered for the draft at the age of 35, just barely getting under the draft limits (18-36).

He trained and was assigned to a hospital group with the 45th Inf. Div. His unit was located just up the slope from the Anzio Beachhead. They were high enough up the ridge to be right under the trajectory, (the pathway) of the big two ton shells that the famous German railroad gun belched out each time it fired. The Germans called it Big Bertha, GIs called it The Anzio Express.

Thurman said when Big Bertha opened up and belched out that two ton projectile it came crashing down on the bay area. The shell made such rumbling noises that you could hear coming for miles around, making the whole bay area tremor and shake like a small earthquake. He said our ships docked along the waterfront and many lined up like setting ducks out in the bay area was under direct fire from Big Bertha. In fact, when the first shell came over his truck he thought the truck was going to take off with them in it. However, after a few more rounds passed over their heads they realized that this was just the beginning of a big duel (gun battle). This gun battle would last out the duration of the Anzio Beachhead Campaign. Thurman's unit would just have to relax and sit tight and weather the storm.

This gun battle became notorious. It was a very dramatic event. Every time the big railroad gun rolled out of the tunnel and fired, it made history. The news went around the world. It became like a cat and mouse game. Our forces were the cat and the Germans were the mouse. The Germans knew they had about 15 minutes to roll out and fire and be back in the tunnel before all hell broke loose on them. Our artillery men were just waiting for the right time to blast away at them with artillery fire. Our artillery men were hoping to cripple the big monster or knock out the rail tracks behind the railroad gun gondola and then have our bomber aircraft come in and finish it off, i.e. "Do the dirty work."

Eventually we caught the big mouse (Big Gun while he was out of his den (tunnel) and our big cats (bombers) jumped on it and ate it alive. This all happened about the time the big push was to come off. Top brass knew that Big Bertha would be doomed sooner or later because the big push north to Rome was imminent. After the breakout that would certainly put Big Bertha to sleep forever.

The 361st Inf. Regt. had just finished training in Africa. They pulled away from the 91st Inf. Div. and were sent to Anzio to re-enforce the 45th Inf. Div. during the breakout from the Anzio Beachhead. R.A. Harper, BAR man with Co. B 361st Inf. Regt., came on line shortly after the breakout. He described the battle for the breakout this way. He said his company was attacking a big rough and rugged hill when his squad, leading the attack, came under heavy machine gunfire from both sides of the hill. One of the German machine gunners opened up on him, ripping his back pack to pieces.

Whoa, that's what I would call a close call. He said he was crawling close enough to the ground for the bullets to pass through his backpack and not his back. He went on to say that he was blessed by having a big boulder out in front of him that he could crawl behind for better protection. Co. B continued attacking the hill and took the pressure off of him and his squad so they could pursue the enemy up the boot of Italy to the Eternal City of Rome.

Chapter 52
TWO GIS WENT OVER THE HILL

Pvt. John Doe Ridge and James Whittle Flatt (names have been changed to prevent embarrassment to them or their family members) were run-away soldiers that went over the hill. John's wound previously from machine gun-fire had shaken him up over that incident. However, James became just plain scared, weak and trembling. He didn't want any part of combat duty. Some would say that James was a yellow bellied coward, and others would say he was a rebellious kid without a cause.

I met James while we were in reserve just behind the front lines in our light artillery sector just before he took off for his second departure. He told me then that he had "had it," just couldn't take it any more and he was stay-ing behind. In other words, he was going over the hill, Absent With Out Leave (AWOL).

John had been wounded before by German machine gunfire, which left him jittery. He had his rifle shot out of his hands and one bullet cut off part of his right thumb. That incident alone seemed to have dampened his desire to attack the enemy head on once again. So John and James became AWOL buddies for the second time.

They were both picked up by the Military Police after they had roamed around the big city of Florence for a couple of weeks. They were both brought to trial and court-martialed. The penalties: (first offense, six months; second offense, 50 years at hard labor; third offense, escape while under guard, car-ries a life sentence). However, they were court-martialed for the second time and both got reduced sentences of six months at hard labor. Both were as-signed to the combat engineers, working up front busting rocks, building roads while under military guard and under the sights of the German 88s.

The first few days while working on the road everything went just fine for them. Then the Germans decided that the GIs were making too much progress on this mountain pass road, so they started shelling the devil out of it with their deadly accurate 88mm artillery fire. As the 88s began to come in, screaming that high pitch vibrant killer sound, and brother, I mean shrilling. It makes a sound that you don't duplicate. Nowhere have I ever heard this sound since. Yes, I mean, nowhere. War movies can't get close to that fearful sound.

The sound of the first 88 exploding nearby caused the military guard to panic and he hit the bar ditch for cover leaving John and James unattended. They decided to make a run for it by hitting the bar ditch on the opposite side of the road bed and went down it until they were out of sight. They were home free they thought. That's when they headed south running off the front lines under guard. They went AWOL for the third time. They were not on the loose for long before being picked up and court-martialed for the third time with a very stiff sentence for James. James got 50 years and was sent to a "Federal Prison Farm" in upper state New York. John's sentence was much more lenient because of his hand wound. His 50 year sentence was rescinded, and he later retrained as an administrative type person and was given a desk job in the rear area.

A couple of months later one of James buddies received a long letter from James giving us the low down on his new lifestyle and also an update on John's new life. James said he was happy where he was, much more than combat duty. He said that his parents had hired a lawyer and were working on getting him out of service with limited disability on his discharge.

You must understand; front line combat duty is different from regular garrison type combat duty. GIs that go AWOL from combat duty are lacking something. They run off of the front lines under fire being very disturbed. They both apprehended court-martials and were sent back to the front for their real punishment. Rear echelon GIs were handled entirely different. If he commits murder, rape, and rapes again, or steals a shipload of cigarettes or booze and gets caught selling it on the black market, he would be in deep trouble. He will be court-martialed and after a long training program be sent to the front lines for his severe punishment. That is, if he's proven guilty of racketeering, and not supporting the enemy war effort.

I remember this one GI that was my foxhole buddy out on the perimeter road, the farthest point out in no-man's land. He was telling me about a wild chase and a firefight he had with the highway patrol outside his hometown in southern Alabama. He had robbed a small town bank and was on the run when word got out that he was notorious, heavily armed and very dangerous. The highway patrol set up a road block just south of town. They had him roped in temporarily until he cut across an open field and hit a dirt road going south. Unfortunately that road led him into a dead end situation.

He lost his last chance of getting away, so he had to make a choice of giving up peacefully or fighting it out with the highway patrol. He chose to fight it out with the patrol officers when they began to close in on him. He pulled his pistol and began to fire, but being out manned, and out-gunned he finally gave up and was captured, convicted of armed robbery, resisting arrest, attempted murder, etc. He was sent to prison for the long haul. "He wasn't exactly a "Machine Gun Kelly," or "Bonnie and Clyde" type desperado, but he was wild enough in his talk and actions to make me wonder, "How in the world did he manage to show up here in my foxhole?"

Now here he was in my foxhole fighting the Germans for his freedom. He said after the war he would be a free person. Whoa, what a choice this man has to become free of his past sins. Now we have James who was fighting the Germans and lost his freedom, because he didn't fight long and hard enough, and now we have this armed robber who will go free after the war. Which of the two GIs do you think should go free, either one or both of them?

Chapter 53
THE LITTLE SPOON

Uncle Sam's large cumbersome mess kit utensils made up of knife, fork, and spoon that wasn't quiet up to par for the front line combat trooper. So the GI had to forage for himself. You understand the large spoon was tremendously large to eat out of a K-ration can, which was a shade larger; or about the size of a potted meat can.

If you didn't have something smaller than the GIs spoon then you had to finger out your greasy meat dishes by hand and wipe your greasy hands on your pants' legs. By the way Uncle Sam didn't send along a roll of paper towels to wipe your dirty hands on either. After two or three weeks of this type housekeeping your pants' legs started to look like a grease monkey (grease rack mechanics) dirty hand towel. The sad part about the mess kit was that we hardly ever got to use them because we were on the move attacking and pushing forward. Most of the time our food was brought up by mule train, and they didn't have room for the mess kit. We certainly didn't want to carry the cumbersome thing on our back. Correction, we did retain the mess kit while in a holding position on the winter watch.

So, K-rations and the little spoon were a perfect match, they just went together, and very seldom did you ever see a GI carrying the big GI spoon in combat. Actually what you saw hanging on his ammunition belt was a small spoon, all types, shapes and sizes. Either the GI bought it at the 5th Army Rest Center or he foraged for it himself up front in a small town or village that we had occupied for a short period of time. I think maybe I bought my first little spoon at Monticatini 5th Army Rest Center. However, I found one I liked better up front in a small village and I gave my old spoon to a new replacement GI. That made him real happy, because when you see the little spoon hanging on a GI's ammunition belt that indicates he is an old trooper and he has been around for a while. Now this new GI had become an old trooper automatically just like the rest of us.

I might as well explain or describe what's inside these K-ration boxes. The greasy meat and vegetable dishes that come inside each little can are our main dish. We opened up these cans with a real small can opener that came in the noon meal box. This little can opener was always Johnny on the spot. It always did the trick because it never failed.

Our Daily Meals
Breakfast: Bacon/ham with scrambled eggs and a small package of instant coffee.

Dinner: Beanie-wieners or corn beef & potatoes and instant lime or orange juice.

Supper: Spam meat and potatoes, or noodles and cheese, bouillon and a chocolate bar.

Also included in our daily diet was a package of chewing gum, hard candy, and a packet of three cigarettes.

These three meal packets (about the size of a box of Cracker Jacks) were vital to us when we were attacking the enemy. They issued these units to us just before we moved into the attack position. Therefore, we knew that our platoon, and squad would be the lead attack force on the enemy position. So we gently dropped them down inside our shirt bosom and let our ammunition belt and extra bandoleers of ammunition hold them in place while we skirmished across no-man's land into enemy territory. The little spoon never declared ever vitally to our needs; therefore, Uncle Sam didn't approve of it so it just faded away after the war.

A package of cigarettes was a must. A big inhaled puff of smoke from a camel cigarette was supposed to settle your nerves while under heavy combat stress. I guess it did the trick, because the first thing we did for a wounded GI was to offer him a puff of smoke from a cigarette. A stick of chewing gum was also a lifesaver. A stick of gum would help keep you from getting thirsty on a long hot day. Even more important, it helped protect your teeth from being shattered from shell concussion.

Chapter 54
GERMAN LIGHT MACHINE GUN

The rapid fire German light machine gun was real light and easy to set up for rapid fire. However, it had its drawbacks because it was hard to hold on target. It would crawl sideways and move upward out of control and was real bad about spitting out all of the ammunition before the gunner realized it all being gone. Another hazard was the barrel would melt down or burn out under continuous firing. However, the assistant gunner normally carried an extra barrel with him that he replaced very rapidly.

I met a young GI that got hit 17 times in the stomach. The bullet holes started around his belly button and moved across his right side, ripping out two rib sections and a kidney before he fell to the ground. He said the bullet holes were so close together they looked like the doctor used a sewing machine stitch to sew him up. He also stated that he considered himself a very lucky person to be alive. If the gunner had started racking him from his left side and moved across his whole body he would have been completely in two pieces.

The light machine gunner didn't have a big devastating effect on our company once he opened up and gave us a chance to locate his position. Sgt. McDermott would disperse the squad just enough to get himself in the right position. After we located the machine gunner he would get picked off by our dead eye sergeant. You could say, wrap him up as a dead duck, please! The individual sharpshooter rifleman (friend or foe) was the main strength of anybody's army.

Chapter 55
BREAKOUT INTO THE PO-VALLEY

The 363rd Inf. Regt. broke out of the Apennine Mountain into the Po Valley running full blast. I remember loading on trucks and heading north to the Po River where we began to see all kinds of burned out German vehicles. They become destroyed right at the water's edge, nobody got away, no bridge to cross, everything that moved was destroyed.

By the time we made it to the river the combat engineers were there to set up a bridgehead for us to cross. They were jolly on the spot. They set up a pontoon bridge for us to cross over the Po River and continue the pursuit of the German army all the way into the city of Udine, Italy. As we moved on farther north we passed people walking along the highway going north. About the time our truck was alongside of an individual, mostly young ladies, the truck driver would turn off the ignition switch. The driver would then turn the key back on causing the truck to backfire with a big bang. The noise sounded just like rifle fire, and the person we were passing would scream out just like they were being shot. Naturally we all got a big laugh out of the loud scream from the young person. "All from the big bang."

We thought the Po Valley was running full of vino (wine) but instead we found none. The valley had turned into the Silk Worm Capital Of The World. The grape vineyards had turned into mulberry tree farms. The wine sellers had changed into high loft barns that housed the large silk worm population that eats the fresh tender leafs off the harvested limbs of the mulberry tree. The silk worm farmer harvested mulberry limbs daily. He carted them directly to the high loft where he neatly spread the branches sparingly over the top of the silk worms. After a couple of days the worms would eat their way up to the new food chain permitting the farmer to remove all of the old branches. This process went on and on until the silk worm finished spinning its cocoon. Then the farmer would harvest the finished product until he had collected a large bag full of silk cocoons and off to market they went.

Our company did without the vino, but we found other things that I liked better. For instance fresh bread, fresh eggs, and fresh ears of corn. Later on we moved up into the high mountain range along the Yugoslavian border, where we began to receive fresh red cherries that Uncle Sam bargained for right off of the Italian economy.

The 363rd Inf. was set up on the outskirts of Udine, Italy for a few days when we got orders to move out to this small village named DeQualls, a small farming district that was devastated by a large hail storm. Our mission was to keep the local farmer in place until emergency relief was brought in. However; as usual, there are some people that just can't sit still. These few families loaded up their belongings and started moving out. That's when the local authorities called on Uncle Sam for help.

Our truck loaded with our squad pulled into this little farm village square where we started to unload our gear, dropping it off at the end of the tailgate. I looked up and noticed this giant-size guy standing there looking right at me. "Wow," I said to him, "You look just like "Primo Canaro?" He said," You're right, sonny. How did you know that?" I told him I had seen his picture in the *Stars and Stripes* newspaper just recently. The paper stated that he had started a new profession as a wrestler. He said, "you're right, and I'm doing just fine in this new job."

We finished our unloading and settled into our new home. Meanwhile Primo called us together and invited us over to his home the next evening. He said he would take us on a tour of his home and boxing arena and we would see his boxing ring just like the one he fought in for the world title. He also showed us all of his mementos that he had collected over the years. Primo showed much courtesy to our unit and was always available to assist us anyway he could.

The next morning our squad went out on the west side of town and set up a road block and started turning families around and sending them back to their homes. We gave them pamphlets advising them what to do to receive hail damage aid benefits from the government. The people seemed satisfied with the instruction we were giving them; in fact, they didn't have any other choice but to hope for the best. Our squad spent nearly two weeks in this little village. Then orders came down for us to move out and pick up our new assignment in the high mountain range where the Italian and Austrian armies fought to a standstill during WWI. Our job was to hold back Marshal Tito's forces that were threatening to take all of the Italian territory from the Yugoslavian border down to the PO-River. This territory included the deep sea port city of Trieste. This was our last combat assignment before we broke camp and headed south on the Italian railroad express on the first leg of our trip home.

Chapter 56
THE TENNESSEE STUD

Henry was assigned to the 3rd Squad of our unit. He became known as Henry the Tennessee Stud. I became acquainted with him during our short stay at the Mussolini Dairy farm on our way home. Henry was rather small in stature, about 5'7 inches tall and weighed in at about 120 pounds soaking wet. He was blond headed and had a rather long neck, just a typical Tennessee mountain man. By him having the long neck we should have called him "pecker neck" for short, but we didn't.

He told me during combat he always carried his slingshot around his neck with a few small rocks in his pocket. He had them ready just in case he needed to use his slingshot to ward off German snipers that seemed to always lurk around his foxhole. I asked him to explain how he used this special weapon on the enemy. Because I was a country boy myself and used the slingshot a lot hunting small game while growing up, I considered myself a pretty good shot. You remember the Biblical story, how David slew Goliath with his slingshot, don't you? So I thought maybe Henry was using his slingshot to slay the Germans like David did.

He explained his encounter with the enemy this way. He said, when the German sniper got close enough to throw rocks or small objects over into his foxhole he knew it was time for him to do something. He knew the sniper was close enough to release a potato masher (hand grenade) over into his foxhole any moment. He also knew the sniper was just waiting outside for him to raise up just enough where the sniper could put a red hole through his head. "And brother, that was a no-no," under this type of circumstance you keep your head down and you will live longer. Fortunately, he said he would load his slingshot and put his miracle weapon to work, and this was the way he did it. He told me that he reached in his pocket and pulled out a small rock about the size of a marble and loaded up his slingshot. He then drew it back while still hunkered in his bunker and release the rock toward the enemy sniper. He said, when the rock fell near the enemy's position, it invariably had some type of effect on him, because in most of his encounters with the enemy he scared him away. However, he did say that sometimes he had to sling out more than one rock to do the job.

This guy really swore by his miracle weapon, because he said that it saved his life many times. Gosh, what a great idea, he might just have something going for him. You know it's possible that a GI can sling a rock out of his foxhole further with this type of weapon than throwing a hand grenade out by hand. Who knows, maybe in some situations the slingshot could be a more effective weapon than the hand grenade. Anyway, I didn't dispute his claim, one "Iota." That's my opinion, what's yours?

Now let's get to the real story about this very peculiar GI Joe, whom I will call Henry, "The Tennessee Stud." This little GI was hung with the largest jock in the Army, and showed it off. He was the biggest show-off in our company and I guess he had that right, because no other person there measured up to the size of his big jock, and it really showed.

I remember the day we had to fall out in the company street for our routine short arm inspection, just a few days before we moved out to board ship on our way home. The doctor came down this long line and had each GI to milk down his jock as he went past. As the doctor passed by each person, the line would bow around just a little more. Everybody in the line wanted to see how the doctor would react when he got down to Henry, "The Tennessee Stud." Finally the doctor made it down to Henry and the doctor stopped and backed off just a little bit and said to Henry, "Where did you get such a big jock as that thing?" Henry as usual let out that high pitched giggle voice of his and said, "Doctor, this thing is hand-raised, and is special to me." Wow, what a true and honest statement he made to the doctor! The doctor only shook his head and moved on to the next patient.

Ho-Hum, what a person, and what a true story this happens to be. Henry's behavior might indicate that he needed his head examined, and too, maybe he was just a pure bred Tennessee mountain man. Other than that obnoxious behavior, he was a very likable person.

Chapter 57
THE YOUNG ITALIAN SHEPHERD BOY

On our second day at Mussolini's Dairy Farm, tragedy was brought to a young Italian shepherd boy. I had just walked outside my tent to get some fresh air and stroll around the area for a little while. I had been here before on my way up to the front lines back in July 1944.

Sudden like, I heard a loud noise that came from across the Volturno River and when I looked up I saw a black puff of smoke rise up. A little later I saw this young boy bending over and then he fell to the ground. He had been grazing sheep right in the middle of this old anti- tank firing range when he came upon this dud anti-tank shell and decided to hit it with his wand. That caused the shell to explode, throwing shrapnel into his body. At first he bent over and stumbled then he fell to his knees, and by that time I knew he was in serious trouble.

This event happened so quickly and I actually didn't know what to do at first. Then I decided to go inside the big tent for help. However, about that time two GIs came out the door into the street where I was and I began to tell them my story, I said, "We need to get the medics quick." "Wow, what a coincidence we are the medics," they said. I asked them, "Can you help the young boy?" They replied, "We are on our way." The two courageous GIs headed to the river as fast as they could, entered the water and swam across.

I watched as far as I could see them by that time of day it was beginning to get dark. It looked like they made the crossing all right and were preparing the boy so they could bring him across the river with them to the dispensary for medical treatment. The sad part of this mercy mission was that I never knew what happened to the young boy. However, I can say this about those two GI medics they certainly earned their good deed for the day. They went beyond the call of duty to save this young boy's life.

To make this event more devastating, we had used this very firing range once before when we were off the front. We had finished firing on the burned out tank, then we were permitted to go up to the tank and look at the damage done to the monstrous Tiger Tank. At that time I noticed all kinds of anti-tank duds lying around and wondered why the Army didn't pick up these shells after each exercise. This incident could have cost Uncle Sam a big bundle of money for the young boy's injuries or death. As we walked past the tank up near the front I noticed where one shell had hit the main drive wheel damaging the hub and on the hub read, "Made In Sweden."

This brought back old memories. I had read about so many bombing raids being made over many of Germanys major cities just to knock out the ball bearing factories. This bombing raid was primarily to destroy their war making capabilities. "Lo and behold," the Country of Sweden was sitting back, taking life easy playing the role of being neutral. Obviously during this time they were furnishing Germany with a most critical item of the war. Ball bearings, the main item that kept the German war machines rolling on the battlefield. Who knows? Sweden could have furnished them the big tanks as well. To destroy ball bearing factories in Germany cost our country many heavy bombers and airmen, and also cost the German civilian population lots of innocent deaths.

I remember this one incident, where a group of German prisoners was sitting together in a group beside a large water fountain, waiting assignment to a work detail. As I walked by them I noticed this one German soldier weeping, and I stopped to ask him, "Why are you weeping?" He told me he had just received word from the war department that his mother and sister had been killed in a bombing raid. He said he became really upset about this because he felt that our bombers killed his family without cause. He said they were at home bothering nobody, just trying to survive this terrible war. "Now they are dead." I told him, Yes; I understand, but you must remember that Hitler started the war and we all had to suffer for that one big reason. After I left him I began to think about the terrible situation the war had left the world in. I just wondered what he thought after he got home and saw all the destruction caused by the war. The death camps set up by his government just to destroy millions of innocent Jewish people, and some German political prisoners. No doubt in my mind, he had plenty to think about. That's my opinion, what's yours?

Chapter 58
ABOARD SHIP GOING HOME

The big ship *Mt. Washington* came into port and docked at the same place we embarked from the year before. We received orders to be ready to board ship in two days. Whoa, that is sweet music to our ears. We are going home at last. There is nothing to stop us now. Wait just a minute, partner, yes things can go wrong if you are not careful.

I just happened to be out on the rough dirt basketball court that afternoon shooting goals when I suddenly stepped on a rough part of the court and turned my ankle severely. Yes, my ankle became swollen and turned black and blue. The leaders running up my leg to my knee turned red and blue. I checked into the dispensary and the doctor had an x-ray taken of my ankle. He told me that I had a fractured ankle and it would be put in a cast. I would be staying in the hospital for at least two weeks, and of all things miss the ship that was taking me home. "Why? I said, to the doctor. He said I wouldn't be able to walk up that gang plank with any type of load on my back. I told the doctor to give me a release right now, because I was walking my way right out of here and no way was I going to miss that ship. I will walk right up that ramp regardless how bad my ankle's swollen. One way or the other, and by the way, I did hobble up that ramp with the help of a couple of buddies. You know that's what the combat buddy system is all about. Help each other survive.

I spent 12 days of misery on that big ship. I was sick as a horse. Every day when chow was called I'd walk over to the staircase and look down into the galley below and that was as far as I could go. When the hot heat and strong smell of food hit me in the face it would turn my stomach upside down. Boy, I was sick. I just couldn't stand the smell of food. "No way," I was a sick GI. I thought maybe it was sea sickness, so I didn't bother checking into the dispensary on sick call. My buddies kept trying to get me to check in on sick call and enjoy the real benefits of life onboard ship. I managed to tough it out and finally the ship reached port. I received my travel orders with 30 days of furlough time and off I went to Oklahoma City, happy as a Jay bird.

Chapter 59
THIRTY DAYS FURLOUGH

I met my spouse Delorah and we began to live it up for 30 short days. After about 10 days at home I became real sick, my stool was white as chalk. I knew something was wrong. So I checked in with my family Doctor and he told me right off what was wrong. I had a severe case of Yellow Jaundice. Its a disease that effects the function of your liver, and if not treated quickly could be life threatening.

The doctor gave me a prescription for medicine that looked like crystallized salt, with a red liquid that requires shaking up vigorously each time you took a dose. You know after 10 more days I began to show a vast improvement. I began to live and be part of the world again. If I had checked into the dispensary on board ship like my buddies wanted me to, I would have been in sick bay for at least 30 days or more. That period of time in sick bay would have prevented me from going home as planned. However, I ducked out of this episode kind of like I did when I sprained my ankle. This time I managed to get off the ship, where in the other case, I managed to get on the ship.

After I completed my 30 day furlough and reported back to Camp Chaffee, I didn't mention my sick spell to anyone. In fact, I went right on to my new assignment without missing a day on sick leave. Camp Chaffee was a short stay. Our next destination was Fort Ruckner, Alabama. I remember being herded on an old dilapidated troop train made up of old Pullman cars that had seats rotten and worn out; they smelt terrible. There was no food or water for a whole day. Many of the troops began to roust about and complained about the poor services and bad facilities. Everybody began to join the complaining group. I thought maybe we would have a big brawl on board this train if the big wigs didn't wake quickly. The fact of the matter is that these old combat troops weren't going to put up with that type of poor service that is.

As the troop train moved into Montgomery, Alabama, the conductor called out over the intercom that we would unload and be fed breakfast on a two hour lunch break. We will eat at a large hotel restaurant across the street from the railroad station. After we made this stop and got our stomach full of chow everybody seemed satisfied. Then we loaded up and were on our way to our temporary assignment for about two weeks at Fort Ruckner, Alabama, and than we would be on the move one more time. This last move took us to Fort Benning, Georgia, the training center for Officer's Candidate Infantry Training and Parachute Jump School.

Since we were combat Infantry soldiers our new assignment was to run

Infantry combat problems for the Infantry Training School. This was a harsh job, but nothing like combat. We got up at five o'clock each morning and had to be out on location by daylight. We started making dry runs on field problems that the new candidates would be observing from the grand stand nearby at about eight o'clock that morning. We ran the same problem over and over every morning for a solid week and then we had the privilege of running something different for another week. This went on for three months and was finally released from Fort Benning, and sent back to Fort Chaffee for final processing and discharge.

While I was at Fort Ruckner I missed my first pay day and then every month thereafter while at Fort Benning, Georgia. I was always the first one in the pay line, just knowing that I was going to get that big lump sum of green back dollars that Uncle Sam was holding back for me. WOW, I became very disappointed when I had to pull back an empty stub each time. The paymaster told me that I had received my pay. He even showed me my signature on the pay roll sheet. Anyway, after complaining to the officials, I rushed over to the Red Cross Center and collected my measly 10 bucks for my monthly wages. I thought I was in bad shape until I ran into Pvt. Eberhart who had missed two months' payments overseas and now had come up short three months in the States just like me.

We both complained, but nobody could come up with the answer. Why are we being short changed? How was our signature getting on the payroll sheet without our knowledge? Even after being discharged I wrote to my Senator and had it investigated, but it came back just about like I expected, telling me that I had signed the payroll sheet. There was nothing they could do but let that payroll shark in the financial department knock down my pay and Pvt. Eberhart's and no telling how many more GIs that we didn't know about. The bad part about this episode was that this guy was getting away with our hard earned money and not even thanking Pvt. Eberhart or me for it. Whoever this person was, he did a smooth job of robbing us, because every time we went before the paymaster we both pulled back a stub, an empty hand.

Chapter 60
FINAL PROCESS AND DISCHARGE

All things were equal in the Army, so here we go for the last time as a GI. I rushed to turn in all my excess equipment before I got my mustering out pay. Because, if you are short any piece of equipment you will lose that amount on your mustering out pay or else you pay out of your pocket.

Since being short changed for the past three months, I wasn't able to pay out of pocket, so I turned in everything early to make sure that I had everything accounted for. You see in the military when you're in crises like this there is a lot of free borrowing to make up for clothing and equipment shortages. The next morning I went for my final physical. I passed everything until I got to the hearing chamber and that was where I flunked the hearing test. I was partially deaf in both ears. The technician asked me if I wanted to file and I told him if I had to stay one more day in this man's army that I would pass. I wanted to leave my part to my buddies who got shot up and suffered more than I did. So I went on my merry way.

I got home and talked to other people about serving in the military and I became amazed at what I heard. My eyes became opened to the fact. I found out to my amazement, that people who had hardly gotten out of the front yard of their home during the war were drawing some type of disability. However, being satisfied with my decision, and very thankful to God who brought me through the thickness of battle without severe injury. I am home now and that is the place I wanted to be in the first place. The place I call "Home Sweet Home." Brother, there is nothing like it, "period," I'll bet my life on it. That's my opinion, what about you?

Chapter 61
Sgt. McDermott's Marksmanship

Sgt. McDermott cut his teeth on the sights of a rifle. He didn't come out of a trick shooting family, the type that used smoke and mirrors to thrill the audience like I once thought. He was only kidding me about that part of his early training.

However, he did say one time that if only he had a penny for every 22 shell he had fired while growing up he knew he would be a wealthy person.

He didn't grow up in a trick shooting family like I first thought. He was still crazy enough about shooting to ask me to throw up a handful of small pebbles for him to burst in the air with his M-1 rifle. He wanted to prove one thing to me that he was still a trick shooter. I refused because I didn't want the Germans disturbed. It was peaceful and quiet that morning and I wanted it to stay that way. This kind of noise would certainly bring down mortar fire and God knows what else.

He said that his early training started out on a BB gun about the age of five, firing at a wooden spool hanging down on a string. He then advanced to moving targets, objects more difficult to hit, shooting while in a swinging motion. He later advanced to a .22 caliber rifle, hitting objects swinging, turning, and objects flying through the air.

This was the shooting phase that he wanted to prove to me that he could still hit a moving target by me throwing up a hand full of pebbles. "No thanks, sergeant," I honored your shooting ability without rousing up the enemy. He became a near professional type marksman, somewhat better than an expert shot on the firing range by the time he was ready for military service.

Uncle Sam selected him to be a medical type soldier and first trained him to become such. They gave him a medical pill bag and taught him how to save lives. He just didn't like that type of military life, so he decided to do something about it.

He went before the commander, the officer in charge and asked for combat duty. He wanted to see the real thing, combat action where you make your shots count. Instead of giving shots, he wanted to fire the shots, putting that little red hole through the enemy. In other words, he volunteered his services to the Infantry. That's what put the finishing touch on Sgt. McDermott's Infantry career.

Chapter 62
ANALYSIS OF THE BATTLE FOR MONTICELLI RIDGE

I truly believe that we missed the real opportunity for a truce settlement when our officer failed to accept the German officer's proposal. We missed our biggest chance when the German officer came over the ridge waving a white flag and bringing with him two other soldiers. One German bent over and limping. Apparently he was a medic since Sgt. McDermott said he had the Red Cross markings on his helmet. The other soldier was a teenage youngster, probably the officer's aid. As they approached our position our officer went out to meet them and shortly after Sgt. McDermott went out to find out what was going on. The two parties met and after having a short discussion and lots of hand waving the three Germans wound up being taken in as prisoners.

Sgt. McDermott returned to his position and I asked him, "What did the German officer want?" I thought he told me this story.

1) Quote: "The German officer wanted to give up his position if we would send an officer and men back with him as a gesture to show good faith." Now others say the German officer just wanted a truce to remove his wounded from the battlefield.

2) Irwin Motner was the wounded GI being helped off of the battlefield by this young German soldier (officer's aid). Motner spoke the same German Austrian dialect as the German youngster. This young German soldier told Motner that they came in to give up their position because our artillery and aircraft had destroyed everything that moved day and night for the last three days. Nothing had gotten through. All the wounded were dying for lack of medical attention. Those that survived were starving to death. Like the German youngster, it had become a hopeless case to continue the fighting. Holy mackerel! I have heard three different stories from different people about this special event. The final outcome of this decision right or wrong will never be totally known. (However, we can offer our comments and form our own opinion, can't we?).

a) First: Here are two reasons. The German officer was close enough to see our foxhole positions. He could go back and take our men in as prisoners and pinpoint our position with artillery and mortar fire.

b) Second: We believed that the Germans still had enough mortar and artillery shells to do extensive damage to our position if we let him go back. Now let's all look at other comments, actions and reasoning in order to make our point.

1) Could the German officer have exposed our position any more than the snipers that roamed freely in our rear area day after day? Don't you know they knew exactly where we had dug in but didn't have the mortar shells to pound our position like they had before.

2) Over 100 Germans lay dead just outside the large underground bunkers on the backside of the ridge. They lay in position just like being lined up to form a massive counter attack when our artillery fire or our rifleman caught them at the right time to save our day.

3) 100 German soldiers or more, lie dead along the highway leading into the fortress. They apparently were wiped out by our artillery fire or rifle fire when they tried to breach the ring of steel that our artillery men had lain down around the backside of Monticelli Ridge. They too met their doomsday.

4) The large truck load of dark German bread being knocked out during this period confirmed they were hungry. The big question still lingers in my mind: Why didn't we take enough of our men back with the German officer, take what few men the officers had left as prisoners, and capture the hill. If we found him as weak as he seemed to be, I think we could have taken the hill and saved the slaughter of our men as they charged up the slope on Monticelli Ridge.

I am sticking with my story that came out of this great battle for Monticelli Ridge. What do you think about the battle, do you agree with me about the outcome?

Chapter 63
HOW MILITARY MEDALS ARE WON

Napoleon Bonaparte once said, "My soldiers will die for medals honoring them. Hitler used medals to exploit his military aggression. In Hitler's army all of his generals and field marshals being honored, one way or another, with Germany's highest honor, The Iron Cross. When a German general, or field marshal being shown in public view you would see that famous Iron Cross hanging around his neck. This medal signified to the world that this general had met all the requirements of being a top notch, high quality, very aggressive, loyal, war-hungry superman general. He will carry out all orders without reservation even unto death.

In the American Army when a soldier was cited for valor in action and given a medal, it was somewhat different than in the German Army. The American soldier would not wear the Medal of Honor around his neck on the battlefield, but Germans did. In fact, Sgt. McDermott captured a German soldier that had an Iron Cross bradded to his uniform. Sgt. McDermott ripped it off and took it as another war souvenir.

Let's look at the basic reason why few persons and officers got their honors on Monticelli Ridge. Pvt. Hendrickson, our BAR man, received a measly Bronze Star for his valor on the ridge. He was in a key position facing the whole German Army during this heated battle for the ridge just as Sgt. McDermott and I was.

Pvt. Hendrickson was cited for firing on the enemy sniper attacking his position during the critical battle for the ridge. He was cited only because Sgt. McDermott was there to confirm his action. For his extraordinary firepower he and Sgt. McDermott and a few others provided to defend this most critical defense position on the Gothic Line are not cited at all.

Capt. Conley, our commander, was cited (Distinguished Service Cross) for his valor during the heat of the battle. He was being cited for being hunkered in his bunker down the hill while organizing what few officers he had left. He was looking for officers to command while the rest of the company was high up on the ridge fighting for their lives, slowly being slaughtered with very little recognition. From day one, the night of the 15 through 17 September, Co. G was outflanked by German snipers. They were infiltrating our lower left flank position by coming around through a deep draw, bypassing Co. B's outpost position that left our total rear area exposed to heavy German sniper fire. Apparently, these snipers were coming through the same gap down below us that this one man army was trying to defend.

Here we have a very peculiar situation where we have members of a mortar crew leaving their mortar position coming forward and fighting as infantrymen. The worst thing ever to happen to a rifle company is when a mortar crew leaves its critical firing position for the lack of ammunition.

During this heroic fighting on Monticelli Ridge, Co. G was taking a terrible pounding from enemy artillery, mortar fire, and being surrounded by enemy snipers suffering heavy loses. Down the hill a short distance we have a single person doing all of these outrageous things like holding off the biggest German counterattack on Monticelli Ridge. He is standing erect in a shallow foxhole while under heavy attack from the enemy killing Germans madly. Credited with 20 dead Germans found in front of his shallow foxhole.

Nobody in Co. G dared to stand up in a shallow foxhole and fire from our position on Monticelli Ridge! Sorry Sir. Nobody survived in a shallow foxhole. I was there with Sgt. McDermott and Pvt. Hendrickson during the heavy fighting for the ridge.

Although, sad as it might be, the two soldiers that received the highest honors, an officer and a private first class, both were in a position much lower down the slope than our squad. They seemed to be in a better position where more soldiers survived the onslaught, and could tell their battle story that perked-up the ears of our high brass and the news media.

The greatest battle ever fought by Co. G was right here on Monticelli Ridge and it was devastating to our company. However, it didn't matter how many sacrifices being made on this ridge. There was not one Silver Star awarded that I'm aware of for gallantry in action for the infantry rifleman ("dead or alive") that served in this battle so heroically.

To prove my point lets look at the statistics reported in the *Infantry Journal Press 1947*. These figures reveal one thing! Officers or individuals in a rifle company or a detachment have the authority to submit requests for "Gallantry in Action." For this reason he must take action to submit the request and send them forward for consideration.

To submit requests reveals one thing. It shows that an officer has a special interest in his individuals troop performances; or does he have a desire to fabricate stories to satisfy his own ego. In other cases some officers wanted to take no action whatsoever.

In other instances, however, some officers might do it too often and others not often enough. Is that the reason why Co. B has the Medal Of Honor and 20 Silver Stars awarded to their fighting men. It's obvious that some companies just don't get recognized like others do! For instance Co. A and Co. C had a below average seven and six Silver Stars awarded respectively. While other companies like Co. I, Co. K and Co. L in the 3rd Bn. all have high marks. Co. K had as many as 15 awards. Does this mean that some companies have officers and men that are just plain weak and trembling while other companies are strong and vigorous and are committed more to do all the heavy fighting. I don't think so! However, these comments are my own opinion. What's yours?

SILVER STAR AWARDS
363rd Infantry Regiment
"For Gallantry in Action"

ITALIAN CAMPAIGN
1944-45

Originations Awards
Total Average   11

Medical Detachments   28   None

Rifle Companies:

1st Battalion	A	7	Low
	B	20	Very High
	C	6	Low
2nd Battalion	E	16	High
	F	5	Very Low
	G	9	Marginal-Two
3rd Battalion	I	14	High
	K	15	High
	L	12	Average + One

DISTINGUISHED SERVICE CROSS
"For Extraordinary Heroism"

Pvt. Howard E. Weaver, Co. F
2d Lt. Russell McKelvey, Co. F
S/Sgt. Robert J. Hutson, Co. F
S/Sgt. Johnny D. Lake, Co. F
Capt. Edward J. Conley, Co. G

Capt. William B. Fulton, Co. K
lst Lt. Leroy A. Bastron, Co. K
S/Sgt. Alexander Greig (Post.), Co. L
S/Sgt. William A. Montooth, Co. L
1st Lt. Harry L. Brown, Co. L

Our squad, 2nd Squad, bore the brunt of the German counterattacks, 16-17 September 1944, that came morning and night like clock work. We suffered more battle fatalities than any other unit, mostly from sniper fire. There were 11 dead, and seven of those were from head wounds. These battle losses being inflicted on our unit before the big attack got underway. What did our platoon get in return, especially Sgt. McDermott? He suffered the agony of battle and the kiss of death for the most of his comrades. Our platoon was the farthest unit up the slope. Yes sir, I mean there's not a single GI in our unit dared to stand up in his foxhole and fire much less walk around and fire. German snipers had us surrounded. The withering machine gunfire continued to rake our foxhole every moment of the day. That machine gunfire enabled the Germans to control our destiny.

I could even say that Sgt. McDermott and Pvt. Clyde Hendrickson our BAR man killed close to a hundred German soldiers or more found on the opposite side of the ridge facing us! However; I believe that story is just a bit out of reason to be true don't you think? Somebody killed them! I might say this: most all the counterattack came from that direction and Sgt. McDermott fired on them many times, stopping them cold.

Co. B suffered a loss of 14 men in the battle for the ridge. Co. E lost seven dead. Co. G lost 25 men the first 15 minutes of the attack, with a total loss of 36 men dead.

So what I am saying to you survivors of Monticelli Ridge is this! No matter how much blood was shed and death sacrificed on this battlefield, sometimes little recognition is being given to those men that suffered the most and did more to defeat the enemy. This is certainly true when there is nobody left to tell the real story. This story is not meant to defuse or take away from the bravery of the men who got full battle recognition. However, after reviewing the battle conditions and comparing them to the sequence of events makes me wonder. I wonder why Co. G didn't get more protective fire support from our comrades dug in along the lower section of the ridge. I feel that Sgt. McDermott and Pvt. Hendrickson didn't get the full honors they deserved. Even so as it may be, they were all heroes in my eyes.

This is my opinion. What's yours?

Chapter 64
WAR AND PEACE

You have read most of the book and have become familiarized with combat conditions and techniques of warfare so now you're ready to qualify yourself as a combat rifleman. If so, are you ready to make war or had you rather stay home and make love?

Answer the following questions? Then determine for yourself.

1) Do you believe that the survival rate of a combat rifleman up front is one out of eight? The other seven men that enter combat will either lose their life or be seriously wounded and declared disabled to perform combat duty.

2) You become pinned down out in no-man's land under heavy enemy small arm's fire, "What would you do?" Would you lie there and get mortared, and not move for five hours, "just play dead," or would you scamper around and crawl out backward hoping that the enemy wouldn't see you on your departure.

3) If your squad attacked a hill and captured it for the night, would you dig your foxhole just deep enough to get by for the night. Maybe dig it deeper to form a defensive perimeter to protect yourself against possible enemy counterattacks and/or heavy artillery shelling?

4) If mother nature calls and you are dug in deep on a hill under heavy enemy fire, what would you do?

a) Relieve yourself in your foxhole and dirty up your mess, or crap, and roll it up in a nice mud blanket and let it lie.

b) Scoop it up with your hands or trenching tool and toss it outside for the garbage man to pick up the next morning.

c) Wait for nightfall and slip out under the cover of darkness and hit the bushes and tell the enemy to hold his fire while you take a crap.

5) If an enemy sniper was lurking just outside your foxhole tossing small rocks into your den, hoping you would get rattled and rise up, how would you handle that situation?

a) Would you hunker in your bunker and toss out a hand grenade in the direction of the sniper, or

b) would you wait and call in for artillery or mortar fire on your position, pinning the enemy down while you rush his position to overpower him?

6) Which of the following actions would you take? Which one do you consider most importantly:

a) Attack a machine gun nest or a bunker by using suppressing artillery fire, or overhead heavy machine gunfire.

b) Wait and let the other attacking squads move up and put flanking fire on the bunker, outflanking the enemy position.

7) If you were up front under enemy mortar fire range and your squad fell out for a 10 minute break, what would you consider doing? Take it easy, or look for a sheltered area, or start digging a fox hole just in case of a mortar attack.

8) Do you think an Infantry soldier should play his hand in the foxhole like a real poker player plays his hand on the poker table?

a) If you are covered; check, hold, don't move, fold, play dead.

b) If you have the right poker hand; bet it all, bluff him out, take the advantage and over power the enemy.

If you have a week hand, fold up, dig deeper and wait for help, because you don't have a Chinaman's chance to survive.

How would you classify yourself under combat conditions;

a) Being a brave soldier, a cool cat under fire?

b) Last but not least, the glory seeker type soldier, the one that wants to be in the middle of everything, but couldn't hit the side of a barn with a baseball bat? OK, Pvt. Bonnie L. Carroll how did you fair on this questionnaire? I am sorry to say sir, but I flunked the test with flying colors.

I dug at least a thousand foxholes from Florence to the outskirts of Bologna, Italy. I spent many hours lying spread-eagle flat on the ground playing dead, waiting for something to happen, other than being shot through the head, or a mortar shell hitting me square in the back.

Yes, I was sweating from head to toe, while lying there trying to root out enough dirt with my nose and chin to hide a little part of my body. Trying to hide my body from enemy bullets that were peppering up the dirt all around my head. Under these circumstances, mister, you'll try to crawl into, or under anything, even the size of a shoe box if one just happens to be available. Its rather an exciting experience, after you get out of the skirmish alive and its all over with, you can tell about it all over again and even laugh. I never overexposed myself for any reason, I only carried ammunition for our one man army, and Sgt. James L. McDermott did the rest.

Blue ribbon panel selection of infantry soldiers.

9) Now we shall let you select by group the top 100 young men for your combat rifle team, BAR, mortar squad and light machine gun teams as follows:

a) 30 soldiers, height 6' 5", weight, 210 lb.

b) 20 soldiers, height 6' 0", weight, 190 lb.

c) 35 soldiers, height 5' 9", weight, 140 lb.

d) 15 soldiers, height 5' 4", weight, 120 lb.

1) Which group do you think will make the best rifleman?

2) Which group do you think will make the best BAR man?

3) Which group do you think will make the best light machine gunner or mortar man?

a) The answer to 1): Uncle Sam in World War II selected riflemen by target score, as long as you could hit the target and qualify as a marksman regardless of how big or small you might be.

b) The answer to 2): Uncle Sam selects a BAR man by target range score also, but it is more difficult to hit the target with a rapid firing BAR than with a rifle.

If you score high marks with the Browning Automatic Rifle (BAR), (Brother, you have special talent). You have the job regardless how big or small you might be. I remember our BAR man was rather small, he fell in the d) category. Although, the BAR was heavier than the Garand rifle, the assistant Bar man usually carried extra ammunition that made up the bar team. At other times he would help the BAR man carry his weapon when he needed extra help. Most BAR men I knew never carried the two legged pod that went on the front of the barrel to help stabilize it when firing. It was entirely to heavy and cumbersome to carry along with the 20 rounds ammo clip, a total of six clips, which was much more important and easier to handle than the two legged pod.

c) The answer to 3): The light machine gunner being selected the same way as the BAR man. But they were thrown into the weapons platoon with the 60mm mortar men. That team makes up the light weapons platoon that's normally dug in behind and around the company commanders headquarters. They play a very vital role in close combat support. They provided overhead machine gun and directed mortar fire on the enemy's position while our company was engaging the enemy in heavy combat.

Our heavy weapons companies being made up of D, H, and M companies. They were positioned much further back and used a heavy 50 caliber machine gun and 81mm chemical mortars. They carry a tremendous wallop when they go into action. These units have proven their effectiveness time and again in close combat.

10). Now let's look at the fire power utilization that we get out of our individual small arms (WWII) equipment. We will take the three major armies and evaluate them individually. (estimated statistics).

a) German infantry foot solder: Individual fire power utilization; rated #1

b) French infantry foot soldier: Individual fire power utilization; rated #2

c) American infantry foot soldier : Individual fire power utilization; rated #3.

Wait! Wait! Just one minute, where did you come up with such a set of figures like these? Please explain! Who says the German infantry soldier uses his equipment any better than the French, or the American soldier. Well sir, this is my own opinion, what's yours?

e) I actually drew these figures out of the "philosopher's hat," based upon a statement made by a high ranking German general being asked this question by one of our prosecutors at the Nuremberg trials. The German general being asked! Quote, "What would it have taken for Germany to defeat the world and win the war? " His reply:

1) German infantry foot soldier.

2) French artillery.

3) American logistic system.

I will say that's not a bad assessment for the reason that Germany lost the war. Another good reason based on the way the German infantry fired their machine pistols and machine guns at night. They used tracer bullets to the fullest extent. In fact they never knew when to close down, they fired all through the night. This fact alone indicated to me that they were not afraid to use their equipment 100%.

f) The big question still remains: How can we get more fire power utilization out of our soldiers?

1) All volunteer army

Select Special Forces: Marines, Paratroopers, Navy Seals, Green Berets, Army Rangers, etc. (all volunteers) no draft.

2) Patriotic forces like the 442nd Combat Team. Who are those 442nd Combat Team members, anyway? These young men with their Japanese ancestral parents being gathered up along the west coast and sent off too special built camps far out in the desert at the beginning of the war with Japan.

This action was necessary to make sure that these Japanese Americans didn't sabotage the war effort. When these young men became of age they volunteered their services to the war effort and their country. They wanted to prove that they were red blooded, true blue Americans just like the rest of the GIs that were serving in uniform up front biting the bullet. This group of young men served in Italy with the 442nd Combat Team. At wars end they were proven to be the most highly decorated units in the United States Army. All of the above comments are my own opinions, what's yours?

Chapter 65
REFLECTION: UNCLE SAM VERSUS GIDEON'S ARMY

During the Battle of the Bulge in WWII, rumors were rampant that there were enough men on unscheduled or absent without leave (AWOL) in the city of Paris, France, to make up a full division. These rumors being dispelled had Uncle Sam doing a better job selecting and managing personnel. If these rumors were true, then our combat capabilities were being severely weakened.

Uncle Sam has a special way selecting his fighting forces in time of war. He calls up everyone, come one come all. When selected and you pass your physical examination, brother, that was all she wrote. You're in the Army, now! It was a fast way to draft up an army. Obviously, it worked. It seemed to have resulted in having a fighting force that seemed to work, but I'm not sure it was as efficient as God's way when he selected Gideon's army. You know the story, but I will render the official Bonnie Carroll paraphrase of this story to get my message across.

God sent a messenger down to Gideon and advised him that his long lost neighbor down the section line had put up a high scaffold in his front yard. On top of it he had made an alter (Baal, the golden calf for all of his friends to worship. Gideon sent word back to God that he would take care of that little situation. Gideon slipped in by night and did his dirty work, destroying the whole mess. In doing this he really stirred up a hornet's nest.

Next morning his long lost neighbor gathered up hordes of men and moved across the Jordan River. They set up camp right next door. Then they began to beat and bang on pot and pans, forged plow shears into spears and swords and they got ready to do battle and make war in a big way. Gideon becomes shaken by the action and built up a large army force. God interceded, and said, "Wake up man. You have to be sensible. You're building up an army for the wrong reason."

"How is that God? I can't believe what I am hearing, Gideon said. "I have already cut my forces in half, and now God, you want me to reduce my men more. Hey man, I can't do that and win. What other choice do I have?"

God said, "Listen to me real carefully Gideon because this is very important to you. Take your men down to the river and let them drink. I will separate the fearful and trembling from the strong." Gideon said. "How God, how? Tell me more."

"Those that lap water like a dog when they drink you shall set aside by himself. The men that lapped up the water putting their hands to their mouth while they were drinking (300 men) shall stay and fight, all the others shall go home."

Gideon said, "Oh my God, there is no way I can defeat my enemy with this measly little force."

God replied, 'Wait just a minute sir.' If you want me to be with you in this mess you better get with the program, clean up your act and do what I tell you. Your warring neighbors are on the rampage. They are terribly noisy. They hoop and holler and beat pots and pans all night long just like the British 8th Army Forces adjacent to our unit did. They are so loud that you can hear them for miles around and they have become easy prey. God told Gideon to prepare his men for battle but Gideon didn't understand how he could do it. Gideon said, 'God, I can't walk into this strong enemy camp and start slapping the enemy in the face and hog tie him without some help.'

God said that he would have to surprise them! Surprise attack them when they are most vulnerable, unstable, when they have their pants down, when asleep[23], or worshipping Baal or having a gala party. When I give you the signal, blow your horns, clap your hands and break your clay pots, man. Blow your horns so loud that the enemy will fall apart and then you go in and take over. That's exactly what Gideon's small army did and they won the battle. Winning the battle was a very simple matter when God was in charge of hand picking the troops, drawing up the battle plan and executing the action. He did a great job! What a beautiful war story this happens to be. I think this same principle would work in today's army if Uncle Sam could do business like that, by just keeping it pure and simple.

When God selected the 300 men for Gideon's army he was looking for the weak and trembling. He knew by eliminating the weak and trembling the rest would be strong. Sgt. McDermott being selected to stay and fight and selected to head up the first platoon. Bonnie Carroll being rejected and sent home.

I've wondered also, why government wasn't able to evaluate a person's work skills any better than they did, placing the person in a job he's suited to perform. In peace time they seemed interested in selecting the top of the class. In time of war it's totally different. The army will usually take you if you can walk. For example, Sgt. McDermott was selected and trained in the medical field (first aid type). He had to go before the commanding officer and ask for a transfer to the Infantry, seeking combat duty. Fortunately, in my opinion, he turned out to be one of the great soldiers of WWII.

Endnotes

1. Sgt. McDermott was the squad leader for 2nd Squad, and the battle of Pisa had just ended. Shortly thereafter, I was assigned to his unit. This was the biggest battle they had fought up to this time, and naturally, I was interested in knowing more about Co. G's battle for the city of Pisa.

2. A booby trap is usually a block of explosive tied to small wire and camouflaged so you can't see it. You trip on the wire causing the trigger to hit a firing cap that explodes the charge near you. In most instances the booby trap's designed to cause personal injury.

3. Henry Ford Bowen, and John R. Burklow went to Co. "E" 363rd Inf. Regt. They were my trainee buddies.

4. About three months before the war ended we got notice that we had a very short time to ship our war booty home. They gave us a form to fill out and I believe we were authorized three articles per person sent only to one address. At war's end Sgt. McDermott had at least 17 German pistols and rifles, and other smaller articles that needed transportation home. He began to scramble around to get enough reliable GIs with addresses that would drop ship his loot to his California address.

5. These new combat boots had cleats all right but they didn't hold in the mud like we thought they should. However, after a couple of day's practices in those narrow cow trails on the muddy slippery slopes of the Apennine Mountains we became used to them and became mobile once again. In the rainy winter months our feet stayed wet all the time and Uncle Sam had to furnish every GI a pair of dry socks and one hot meal every day while up front (and that was a promise). Socks and hot food came by mule train like all essential items that's required to support the front line mountain fighter.

6. The two young German paratroopers survived that ambush and also the war. We did too, so that makes both parties happy.

7. "Kilroy was here," a hand scribbled marked statement that a GI left behind indicating he was the first person to be in this remote ungodly place.

8. The death angel must have told my little ego sensor to move out of this place, so I took heed to the warning just like being told. Thanks angel.

9. The new lieutenant was dead, so we canceled out the poker game in his honor. Note: Second lieutenants are platoon leaders in a rifle company and go for a dime a dozen. Sorry, but they just don't last very long in a rifle company.

10. Capt. Conley was to busy hunkered in his bunker looking for officers to command to really observe what was going on up where we were. The only bad thing about this heroic action performed by Sgt. McDermott when he has no platoon officers left alive to tell the story. The only other two persons left alive in our squad are Pvt. Bonnie L. Carroll and Pvt. Hendrickson, our BAR man.

11. Knife, Uncle Sam didn't furnish the GI with a dagger type knife like this one. However, a lot of GIs carried them on their ammo belt. The GI found them very useful for opening up of large containers and even cutting up things.

12. "Honey pit" is a dirt or concrete tank dug in the ground adjacent to the barn to catch the run off of human and cattle urine and the solid waste materials from both sources. The farmer in the early spring pumps the liquid waste into a medium size two wheel wooden barrel container wagon. He hooks up his two big white oxen to the wagon and away he goes to the field. As he guides his wagon team down the tilled rocky mountain slope he opens the wooden petcock valve and lets the stinky liquid flow out slowly. He takes the solid waste mixed with hay and loads it on a flat bed wagon and spreads it by hand.

13. A land mine (shu-mine) blast will take off your foot around the ankle and will cause severe pain. Due to the extreme heat coming from the blast it will sear over the wound and greatly reduce the loss of blood. Shrapnel wounds are clean cut wounds. The heat that burns and sears over the other type wound is lost here, causing a much greater loss of blood that can be devastating to a GI lying out on the battlefield.

14. I am making this comment about Sgt. McDermott's statement because of all the hardship and trauma a person goes through upon the front lines. Some GIs are always griping and complaining about combat conditions. This statement was unusual for him to make because he was a real seasoned infantry combat soldier that liked combat. This was the only time I ever heard him say or have any inkling that he would like to be home or even off the front lines.

15. Pleasure house. No, it's not a whorehouse; it's any type structure that is available up front where a squad of men can get inside and be protected from machine gun or mortar fire and surely from German 88s. The time in reserve while waiting to be committed to battle is the time I call pleasure time.

16. It was difficult for a German soldier to give up right after a broadcast. The German officer in charge was watching every soldier's movement very closely.

17. The British 8th Army was always on the east side of us, and occasionally our unit would butt up against them. The 8th Army being made up of troops from all over the Commonwealth.

18. The war was over now but I had remembered Loiano as a town of complete destruction nothing but rubble. When I returned in 1958 the town was completely rebuilt. Everything looked brand new. Nothing looked like the old town.

19. To measure a GI's up front personal carrying capacity, you can use this rule to determine the size and weight. If the item is larger than grandma's snuff boxes and weighs more than a small bar of soap, then the item is too large and heavy to carry. So mom, pop and friends take notice, don't send it. I know just how mom and pop felt about their son's needs up front. As usual, they wanted to give just a little more to their combat warrior. Nevertheless, the same thing applies today as yesteryears.

20. Approximately 10 miles south of Loiano an old sign read, TEDESCO meaning German in Italian. Down the dirt road about 100 yards from this building was a small graveyard, still there with two dozen or more German

dead bodies that nobody ever claimed. At least the German Government would not claim them.

21. This was a promise from Uncle Sam. He promised to deliver hot chow and dry socks every night during the harsh winter months to ever combat infantry soldier while in a holding position. This story sounded like we were a bunch of spoiled brats at first, didn't it? You pull front line duty during the harsh winter months and you will change your attitude real quick.

22. Brenner Pass, gateway into the Po-Valley leading out of Austria and Germany. Brenner Pass being the main supply route for the German war effort going into northern Italy being constantly bombed by our forces.

23. Asleep. This type of warfare has a devastating effect on the enemy, because they never know when being hit next. You know this continued threat of having your throat cut while you're sleeping can be very disturbing. Especially when you're trying to get some of that much needed sleep that goes along with front line duty.

That Old "Fir Tree, What It Means To Me"

That grand old unit is dear to me.
    The Ninety First Division and that old Fir Tree.
History is filled with it's heroic deeds.
    Of gallantry, bravery and loyalty it reads.

Through World War I and the miseries of France.
    When other bogged down we still would advance.
When the battle was over, high above the debris.
    Stood the soldiers that wore that old Fir Tree.

In Africa, it was Oran, Arzue and Ranger Beach.
    And Rommel's tanks left in the sun to bleach.
From the war in Italy came the cry of despair.
    General Clark called for us, he needed us there.

Cities like Anzio, Cecina, Naples and Rome.
    We were battle hardened now and far from home.
Do what others couldn't do, go where others couldn't go.
    Take Leghorn, take Pisa and cross the Arno.

Mountains, mud and the miseries of war.
    Loneliness, death and fear never felt before.
In the toughest places you could ever be.
    They called on the men who wore the Fir Tree.

Mt. Calvi, Monticelli and Hitler's best men.
    The Gothic Line Battle was about to begin.
Probably the hardest battle of World War II.
    But the Ninety First was there to see it through.

Four days of hell on Monticelli hill.
    When it was all over the world stood still.
No machine-gun fire, no artillery burst.
    On top of Monticelli stood the Ninety First.

We spilled our blood on each mountain side.
    In every peak and valley, some of our men died.
Tears came hard for tough men of pride.
    But for every man we left, each one of us cried.

There in Florence long rows of white crosses stand.
    Where we left a friend in a foreign land.
From those rugged hills, his blood cries to me.
    He says, "I lay here so the world can be free."

The friend that died on that Italian hill.
    We have not forgotten and we never will.
As we gather here, old acquaintances to renew.
    His spirit lives as part of you.

The Ninety First Division, the old Fir Tree.
    All these years has been a part of me.
With the coming of winter when chilly winds blow.
    I remember the Apennines and the soft white snow.

To do it all over again, to make the decision.
    I would be a part of the Ninety First Division.
I would wear the symbol of that old Fir Tree.
    And wear it with pride for every man to see.

So walk with pride with that green ribbon on your chest.
    You are the Ninety First, you're one of the best.
When men ask, "Why so proud your buttons would burst?"
    Reply, "Brother, I am a member of the famous Ninety First."

> When this life is over and closes for me.
>   I want it remembered, I wore that Fir Tree.
> I want it said and want it written down too.
>   "Member of the Ninety First Division, World War Two."

Printed by permission March 1997   *by SSgt "Bud" Beeson*
                                      Co. E 363-91-WWII

157

Index

Printed in the USA
CPSIA information can be obtained
at www.ICGtesting.com
JSHW082346140824
68134JS00020B/1908

9 781681 624075